KETO DIET
MEDITERRANEAN
Cookbook for Beginners

Easy Mediterranean Recipes with 14-Day Meal Plan for Anyone on Keto Diet

Silvia Cerroni

Copyright © 2019 by Silvia Cerroni

All rights reserved worldwide.

ISBN: 978-1092402286

No part of this book may be reproduced or transmitted in any form or by any means, electronic or mechanical, including photocopying, recording or by any information storage and retrieval system, without written permission from the publisher, except for the inclusion of brief quotations in a review.

Warning-Disclaimer

The purpose of this book is to educate and entertain. The author or publisher does not guarantee that anyone following the techniques, suggestions, tInstant Pots, ideas, or strategies will become successful. The author and publisher shall have neither liability or responsibility to anyone with respect to any loss or damage caused, or alleged to be caused, directly or indirectly by the information contained in this book.

CONTENTS

INTRODUCTION 7
KETOGENIC DIET - THE NEW LIFESTYLE 8
WHAT IS THE MEDITERRANEAN DIET? 14
BREAKFAST 16
Cinnamon Waffles with Cheesy Spread 16
Salmon, Cream Cheese & Dill Pinwheels 16
Spinach Nested Eggs 17
Power Avocado-Berry Smoothie 18
Almond Flour Crepes with Rasberry Sauce 18
Cheese & Prosciutto Frittata 19
Carrot Zucchini Bread 20
Pistachio & Mascarpone Pots 20
Mozzarella & Chistorra Spanish Chorizo Omelet 21
Morning Buttered Eggs 21
Nut Granola with Yogurt Smoothie 22
Smoked Salmon & Mascarpone Omelet Roll 22
Egg & Aioli Salad 23
Breakfast Almond Milk Shake 23
Zucchini Patties with Pancetta 24
Mozzarella & Broccoli Scramble 24

LUNCH RECIPES 25
Lettuce & Endive Tuna Salad 25
Mediterranean Salad 25
Baked Italian Sausage with Cheese Topping 26
Butternut Squash Stuffed with Beef & Mushrooms 26
Chicken Lettuce Wraps 27
Prawn & Arugula Salad 28
Roasted Pork with Green Sauce 28
Vegetable Frittata 29
Anchovy Caprese Salad 29
Minty Pesto Rubbed Pork Chops 30
Juicy Pork Chops with Olives 30
Ground Beef with Cauliflower and Cabbage in Oven 31
Oregano Tomato Cream Soup 31
Homemade Rolled Porchetta Roast with Pine Nuts 32
Pork Sausage & Pancetta with Kale 32
Summer Spanish Gazpacho with Ricotta Cheese 33

Classic Greek Salad 33
Caesar Salad with Smoked Salmon and Poached Eggs 34
Greek Moussaka 34
Mixed Grilled Vegetables with Beef Steaks 35
Gorgonzola & Pancetta Green Salad 36
Tasty Dijon Pork Chops 36
Easy Green Soup 37
Dilled Baby Artichoke Salad 37
Veggie and Pork Osso Bucco 38
Cauliflower Cream Soup with Pancetta & Chives 38
Balsamic Glazed Beef Meatloaf 39
Turkey Pizza with Pesto Topping 40
Zucchini Frittata with Tomato & Bresaola Salad 41
Broccoli Cheese Soup 42
Baked Pork Sausages 42
Parsley Beef Meatballs with Marinara Sauce 43
Fried Cod with White Wine Sauce 44
Feta & Zucchini Gratin 44
Anchovy Caesar Salad 45
Pancetta and Green Veggie Gratin 46
Herby Salmon with Creamy Sauce 46
Almond-Crusted Salmon 47
Tuscan Salmon Salad 48
Baked Fish with Parmesan Topping 48

SNACKS 49

Homemade Biscuits with Mascarpone Snap 49
Chicken Fritters with Rosemary Dip 50
Cheesy Crackers 50
Crispy Zucchini Sticks 51
Parsley & Garlic Celeriac Mash 52
Green Bean Crisps 52
Greek Zucchini Chips 53
Mascarpone & Bresaola Roll 53
Ricotta Filled Piquillos 54
Mozzarella Biscuits 54
Effortless Spinach Balls 55
Stuffed Avocado with Tuna 55
Feta Balls with Spring Salad 56
Arugula & Ricotta Gnocchi 56
Mushroom Cheesy Balls 57
Herby Stuffed Eggs 58
Meaty Vegetable Tart 58

Catalan Salsa Aioli 59
Scallions and Cheese Stuffed Tomatoes 59
Mascarpone & Carrot Mousse 60

DINNER RECIPES **61**

Mediterranean Chicken Breasts 61
French Chicken Packets 62
Spanish Chorizo Chicken Paella 62
Tomato and Eggplant Braised Chicken Thighs 63
Lemon-Marinated Chicken Kebabs 64
Veggie Chicken Drumsticks with Tomato Sauce 64
Turkey Meatballs with Squash Pasta 65
Bresaola & Gorgonzola Cakes 66
Chicken Breasts Stuffed with Parma Ham 66
One-Pot Chicken and Broccoli 67
Gorgonzola Stuffed Bell Peppers 68
Chicken Wings with Parmesan & Yogurt Sauce 68
Grilled Asparagus with Pancetta Wrapped Chicken 69
Spring Omelet 70
Omelet Flambé 70
Five Spices Chicken Kabobs 71
Cheese Turkey with White Sauce 71
Stuffed Chicken Breasts with Basil Tomato Sauce 72
One-Pot Rosemary Chicken Thighs 72
Herbs Stuffed Roast Chicken 73
Chili & Sage Flattened Chicken 73
Turkey Soup with Zoodles 74
Cheesy Spinach Chicken Bake 74
Delicious Chicken Goujons 75
Marvellous Turkey Meatballs 75
Mustard Chicken Thighs 76
Baked Breaded Chicken 76
Turkey Bacon & Broccoli Pancakes 77
Zucchini Noodles with Turkey & Bolognese Sauce 78
Spanish Chicken with Tomate Sofrito Sauce 78
Baby Spinach and Cheese Stuffed Chicken Breasts 79
Four-Cheese Chicken with Pancetta and Zucchini 80
Sautééed Pork Lettuce Cup Wraps 80
Greek-Style Chicken with Olives and Capers 81
Speedy Tilapia with Tomato Sauce & Olives 81
Minty Pork Balls with Fresh Salad 82
Traditional Bolognese Sauce 82

Baked Zucchini Stuffed with Shrimp & Dill 83
Garlic Chicken with Anchovy Paste 84
Sardines Skillet with Zucchini Spaghetti 84
Buttered Garlic Shrimp 85
Cheesy Salmon with Crème Fraîche Spread 85

MEATLESS MEALS 86

Goat Cheese Frittata with Bell Peppers 86
Creamy Vegetable Stew 86
Spinach & Feta Lasagna 87
Eggplant Dipped Roasted Asparagus 88
Steamed Asparagus & Grilled Cauliflower Steaks 88
Green Bell Pepper & Mushroom Stew 89
Mushroom Cheeseburgers 90
Traditional Spanish Pisto 90
Green Beans & Sage Flan 91
Classic Greek Salad with Dill Dressing 92
Zucchini Spaghetti with Avocado & Capers 92
Vegan Minestrone 93
Cauliflower & Kale Cheese Waffles 93
Classic Pizza Margherita the Keto Way 94
Charred Asparagus with Creamy Sauce 94
White Cabbage with Parmesan 95
Cauliflower Patties 96
Tumeric Baked Vegetables 96
Cheesy Spaghetti Squash 97
Vegan Cheese Stuffed Zucchini 98
Kale & Cauliflower Soup 98
Creamy Avocado Carbonara 99

DESSERTS 100

Macadamia Ice Cream 100
Cardamom Cookies 100
Keto Creme Caramel 101
Dark Chocolate Hazelnut Chocolate Bark 102
Hazelnut Truffles with Berry 102
Mini Chocolate Cheesecakes 103
Chocolate Pudding in a Mug 103
Fluffy Chocolate Mousse with Strawberries 104
Cashew Cakes 104
Speedy Fat Bombs 105

14-DAY MEAL PLAN TO LOSE UP TO 20 POUNDS 106

INTRODUCTION

Want to follow a ketogenic diet but not sure where to start? Struggling with finding delicious and tummy-filling recipes when going "against the grains"? Do not worry! This book will not only provide you with fantastic keto recipes that will get you started in a jiffy, but it will also teach you the ultimate tricks for adopting a keto lifestyle forever.

Mouth-watering delights for any occasion and any eater, you will not believe that these recipes will help you restore your health and slim your body. Ditching carbs do not mean ditching yummy treats, and with these original recipes, you will see that for yourself.

Successfully practiced for more than nine decades, the ketogenic diet has proven to be the ultimate long-term diet for any person. The restriction list may frighten many, but the truth is, this diet is super adaptable, and the food combinations and tasty meals are endless.

Try these delicacies and see what I am talking about.

KETOGENIC DIET – THE NEW LIFESTYLE

It is common knowledge that our bodies are designed to run on carbohydrates. We use them to provide our bodies with the energy required for normal functioning. However, what many people are clueless about is that carbs are not the only source of fuel our bodies can use. Just like they can run on carbs, our bodies can also use fats as an energy source. When we ditch the carbs and focus on providing our bodies with more fat, we are embarking on the ketogenic train.

Despite what many people think, the ketogenic diet is not just another fad diet. It has been around since 1920 and has resulted in outstanding results and amazingly successful stories. If you are new to the keto world and have no idea what I am talking about, let me simplify this for you.

For you to truly understand what the ketogenic diet is all about and why you should choose to follow it, let me first explain what happens to your body after consuming a carb-loaded meal.

Imagine you have just swallowed a giant bowl of spaghetti. Your tummy is full, your taste buds are satisfied, and your body is provided with more carbs than necessary. After consumption, your body immediately starts the process of digestion, during which your body will break down the consumed carbs into glucose, which is a source of energy your body depends on. So one might ask, "What is wrong with carbs?" There are some things. For starters, they raise the blood sugar, they make us fat, and in short, they hurt our overall health.

So, how can ketogenic diet help?

A ketogenic diet skips this process by lowering the carbohydrate intake and providing high fat and moderate protein levels. Now, since there is no adequate amount of carbs to use as energy, your liver is forced to find the fuel elsewhere. And since your body is packed with lots of fat, the liver starts using these extra levels of fat as an energy source.

THE KETOSIS

Once your liver begins preparing your body for the fuel change, the fat from the liver will start producing ketones – hence the name KETOgenic. What glucose is for the carbs, the ketones are for the fat, meaning they are the tiny molecules created once the fat is broken down to be used as energy.

The switch from glucose to ketones is something that has pushed many people away from this diet. Some people consider this to be a dangerous process, but the truth is, your body will run just as efficiently on ketones as it does on glucose.

Once your body shifts to using ketones as fuel, you are in the state of ketosis. Ketosis is a metabolic process that may be interpreted as a little 'shock' to your body. However, this is far from dangerous. Every change in life requires adaptation, and so does this.

This adaptation process is not set in stone, and every person goes through ketosis differently. However, for most people, it takes around two weeks to adapt the new lifestyle fully.

Just remember, this is all biological and completely healthy. You have spent your whole life packing your body with glucose; it is only natural that you need time to adapt to the new dietary change.

THE BENEFITS OF KETO DIET

Even though it is still considered 'controversial,' the ketogenic diet is the best dietary choice one can make. From weight loss to longevity, here are the benefits that following a ketogenic diet can bring to your life:

Loss of Appetite

Cannot tame your cravings? Do not worry. This diet will neither leave you exhausted nor with a rumbling gut. The ketogenic diet will help you say no to that second piece of cake. Once you train your body to run on fat and not on carbs, you will experience a drop in your appetite that will work magic for your figure.

Weight Loss

Since the body is forced to produce only a small amount of glucose, it will also be forced to lower insulin production. When that happens, your kidneys will start getting rid of the extra sodium, which will lead to weight loss.

HDL Cholesterol Increase

While consuming a diet high in fat and staying clear of the harmful glucose, your body will experience a rise in the good HDL cholesterol levels, which will, in turn, reduce the risk for many cardiovascular problems.

Drop in Blood Pressure

Cutting back on carbs will also drop your blood pressure. The drop in blood pressure can prevent many health problems such as strokes or heart diseases.

Lower Risk of Diabetes

Although this probably goes without saying, it is important to mention this one. When you ditch the carbs, your body is forced to lower the glucose productivity significantly, which leads to a lower risk of diabetes.

Improved Brain Function

Many studies have shown that replacing carbohydrates with fat as an energy source leads to mental clarity and improved brain function. This is yet another reason why you should go keto.

Longevity

I am not saying this diet will turn you into a 120-hundred-year-old monk. However, it has been scientifically proven that once the oxidative stress levels are lowered, the lifespan is extended. And since this diet can result in a significant drop in the oxidative stress levels, the corresponding effect it could have on a person's lifespan is clear.

THE KETO PLATE

First of all, just because it is called a 'diet' does not mean you are about to spend your days in starvation. The ketogenic diet will neither tell you not to eat five times a day if you want to nor will it leave your belly empty.

The only rule the keto diet has is to eat fewer carbohydrates, more foods that are high in fat, and consume a moderate protein intake. But how much is too much and what is the right amount? The general rule of a thumb is that your daily nutrition should consist of:

65-70 % fat

25-30 % protein

5 % carbohydrates

Or, to be more precise, it is not recommended that you consume more than twenty grams of carbs when on a ketogenic diet.

This macronutrient percentage, however, can be achieved in whichever way you and your belly are comfortable with. For example, if you crave a carb meal now and want to eat, for instance, sixteen grams of carbs at once, you can do so as long as your other meals do not contain more than four grams of carbs combined.

Some of the recipes in this book offer zero grams of carbs, while others have a few grams. By making a proper meal plan that works for you, you can easily skip the inconvenience cloaked around this diet and start receiving the fantastic benefits.

WHAT TO AVOID

To stay on track with your Keto diet, there are certain foods you need to say farewell to. Go to your kitchen and get rid of these tempting but super unhealthy ingredients:

Starchy Vegetables. Potatoes, beans, parsnips, legumes, peas, and corn are usually packed with tons of carbs, so they should be avoided. However, sneaking some starch when your daily carb limit allows is not a sin.

- Sugar
- Grains. Rice, wheat, and everything made from grains such as pasta or bread.
- Trans fats
- Refined Oils and Fats (corn oil, canola oil, etc.)
- Diet Soda

WHAT TO EAT

You can eat anything besides what is mentioned above; however, there are certain foods that will help you up your fat intake and provide you with more longer-lasting energy:

- Avocados
- Whole Eggs
- Meat
- Bacon Fish and Seafood
- Sausage
- Seeds
- Leafy Greens
- Non-Starchy Vegetables: Asparagus, Cucumber, Zucchini, Broccoli, Onion, Cabbage, Tomatoes, Eggplant, Sea Weed, Peppers, Squash
- Full-Fat Dairy (heavy cream, yogurt, sour cream, cheese, etc.)
- Nuts. Nuts are packed with healthy fats, but be careful when consuming pistachios, chestnuts, and cashews, as they contain more carbs than the rest of the nuts. Macadamia nuts, pecans, and almonds are the best for the Keto diet.

KETO SWAPS

Just because you are not allowed to eat rice or pasta doesn't mean you have to sacrifice eating risotto or spaghetti. Well, sort of. For every forbidden item on the keto diet, there is a healthier replacement that will not contradict your dietary goal and will still taste amazing.

Here are the last keto swaps you need to know to overcome the cravings quicker and become a Keto chef:

Bread and Buns - Bread made from nut flour, mushroom caps, cucumber slices

Flour - Coconut flour, nut flour

Wraps and tortillas - Wraps and tortillas made from nut flour, lettuce leaves, kale leaves

Pasta and spaghetti - Spiralized veggies such as zoodles, spaghetti squash, etc.

Rice - Cauliflower rice (ground in a food processor)

Mashed potatoes - Mashed cauliflower or other veggies

Hash browns - Cauliflower or spaghetti squash

Lasagna Noodles - Zucchini or eggplant slices

Bread crumbs - Almond flour

Pizza crust - Crust made with allowed flour, cauliflower crust

Potato chips - Zucchini chips, kale chips

Croutons - Bacon bits, nuts, sunflower seeds, flax crackers

French fries - Carrot sticks, turnip fries, zucchini fries

WHAT IS THE MEDITERRANEAN DIET?

The Mediterranean diet is a combination of food patterns that are complemented by the practice of physical exercise and the climate of the countries around the Mediterranean Sea, and therefore has multiple health benefits.

Regarding food, the Mediterranean diet is based on the ingredients of local agriculture in countries with a Mediterranean climate, mainly Greece, Spain and Italy. It is based on reducing the consumption of red meats and carbs for the benefit of more plant foods and healthy fats, such as olive oil.

Basic foods that make it up

Some of the recommended ingredients are legumes and vegetables, fish, fruit, poultry, pasta, rice and nuts, in addition to the consumption of red wine in moderation. But the most recommended product by far is the olive oil, which thanks to oleic acid and its fats of vegetable origin decreases the risk of obstructing the arteries, and has a high content of carotenes and vitamin E. The Mediterranean diet promotes consumption of olive oil against other types of oil and especially against butter. In this food pattern there is a scarcity of products such as red meat, sweets and eggs.

The Mediterranean diet also takes into account the typical recipes of these places, made with seasonal products, as well as traditional cooking methods and other cultural factors such as the habit of shared meals with family or friends, traditions and celebrations.

Health benefits

The health benefits of this diet are more significant when combined with physical exercise. This should be moderate, but if possible it should be done for at least 30 minutes a day, five days a week. Or if you have difficulties doing that, it should be done as regularly as possible. Options like brisk walking, running, swimming or cycling are advisable, but you can also resort to any other sport or activity that helps burn calories and fat, as well as optimal physical maintenance. Thus, it contributes to lose weight, control blood pressure and hypercholesterolemia, and delay cognitive deterioration. The usual practice of physical exercise also offers protection against chronic diseases such as diabetes or Alzheimer's.

The Mediterranean diet not only helps control weight and increase the sense of physical well-being, but it also improves the functioning of various organs, such as the heart and the kidney. It has also been found that the countries around the Mediterranean Sea have among the highest life expectancy in the world with Spain, Italy and France all being part of the longest living nations.

This food pattern, which has been passed on from generation to generation over many centuries, has evolved and welcomed new types of foods and different ways of preparation, but maintains the properties and characteristics that model a healthy and easy lifestyle people of all ages and physical conditions can practice. The products are widely available and quick to prepare, and there are lots of recipes, simple and more complex, with which to get the most out of the Mediterranean diet. In addition, its importance in the welfare of individuals is not limited to the fact that it is a varied, healthy and balanced diet; also keep in mind that its low content of saturated fats and sugars, and its abundance of vitamins and fiber contribute to its richness in antioxidants.

Risks of the Mediterranean diet

Despite its many advantages, going after the Mediterranean diet can reduce iron and calcium levels caused by the reduced consumption of meat and dairy products. That's why I recommend that you consult your doctor or nutritionist if you have to take additional supplements to improve the levels of these minerals. As for the wine, it is better to take it during meals, but know it's not essential, so it can be avoided if it there is a risk to your health.

BREAKFAST

Cinnamon Waffles with Cheesy Spread

Total Time: 25 minutes | Serves: 6

Per serving: Calories 495, Fat 48.5g; Net Carbs 2.8g; Protein 13g

Ingredients

7 large eggs
5 tbsp olive oil, melted
1½ cups almond milk, unsweetened
¼ tsp liquid stevia
½ tsp baking powder
1½ cups almond flour
8 oz cream cheese, at room temperature
1 tsp cinnamon powder
3 tbsp swerve brown sugar
Cinnamon powder for garnishing

Directions

Whisk the olive oil, almond milk, and eggs in a medium bowl. Add the stevia and baking powder and mix. Stir in the almond flour and combine until no lumps exist. Spritz a waffle iron with cooking spray.

Ladle a ¼ cup of the batter into the waffle iron and cook until golden, about 10 minutes in total. Repeat with the remaining batter.

Combine the cream cheese, cinnamon, and swerve with a hand mixer until smooth. Cover and chill until ready to use.

Slice the waffles into quarters; apply the cheesy spread in between each of two waffles and snap. Sprinkle with cinnamon powder and serve.

Salmon, Cream Cheese & Dill Pinwheels

Total Time: 10 min + cooling time | Serves: 3

Per serving: Calories 250, Fat 16g; Net Carbs 7g; Protein 18g

Ingredients

3 oz cream cheese, softened
Zest and juice of 1 small lemon
3 tsp fresh dill, chopped
Salt to taste
3 oz smoked salmon, sliced

Directions

In a bowl, whisk the cream cheese, lemon juice, and salt until smooth and fluffy. Fold in the dill and lemon zest. Lay each salmon slice on a plastic wrap and spread with cheese mixture.

Roll up the salmon and secure both ends by twisting. Refrigerate for 2 hours, remove plastic, and cut into thick slices to serve.

Spinach Nested Eggs

Total Time: 37 minutes | Serves: 4

Per serving: Calories 230, Fat 17.5g; Net Carbs 4g; Protein 12g

Ingredients

2 tbsp Pecorino Romano cheese, shredded
2 tbsp gouda cheese, shredded
1 tbsp olive oil
1 clove garlic, grated
4 cups spinach, chopped
Salt and black pepper to taste
4 eggs

Directions

Warm the oil in a skillet over medium heat; add the garlic and sauté until softened for 1 minute. Add the spinach to wilt for about 5 minutes, and season with salt and black pepper. Allow cooling.

Grease a baking sheet with cooking spray, mold 4 spinach nests on the sheet, place in each one Pecorino Romano and gouda cheese, then crack an egg into each nest. Season with salt and black pepper.

Bake for 15 minutes at 350°F just until the egg whites have set and the yolks are still runny. Plate the nests and serve right away.

Power Avocado-Berry Smoothie

Total Time: 5 minutes | Serves: 3

Per serving: Calories 463, Fat 38.7g; Net Carbs 10.7g; Protein 6.8g

Ingredients

1½ cups unsweetened cashew milk
1 avocado, pitted and sliced
3 cups mixed berries (of choice)
6 tbsp heavy cream
2 tsp xylitol
1 cup ice cubes
¼ cup nuts and seeds mix

Directions

Combine the berries, avocado slices, cashew milk, heavy cream, xylitol, ice cubes, nuts and seeds in a smoothie maker; blend in high-speed until smooth and uniform. Pour the smoothie into drinking glasses, and serve immediately.

Almond Flour Crepes with Rasberry Sauce

Total Time: 15 minutes | Serves: 4

Per serving: Calories 425, Fat 34.1g; Net Carbs 4.8g; Protein 9.8g

Ingredients

Crepes
1 cup almond flour
½ tsp salt
2 drops liquid stevia
1 tsp baking powder

1 cup almond milk
4 large eggs
2 tbsp olive oil
1 tsp vanilla extract

Raspberries Sauce
3 cups fresh raspberries
Juice of ½ lemon
6 drops liquid stevia

½ cup water + 1 tbsp water
½ tsp arrowroot starch

Directions

In a bowl, mix the almond flour, salt, stevia, and baking powder with a whisk, and set aside. In another bowl, whisk the almond milk, eggs, and vanilla extract together.

Then, pour the egg mixture into the almond flour mixture and continue whisking until smooth.

Preheat the griddle pan over medium heat and grease with olive oil.

Pour 1 soup spoonful of crepe batter into the griddle pan. Cook on one side for 2 minutes, flip the crepe, and cook the other side for 1 minute until brown and crispy.

Transfer the crepe to a plate and repeat the cooking process until the batter is exhausted.

Pour the raspberries and half cup of water into a saucepan, and bring the berries to boil over medium heat, for about 8 minutes. Lower the heat and simmer the berries for 5 minutes so that they are soft and exuding juice. Pour in the stevia at this point, stir, and continue cooking for 5 minutes.

Next, stir in the lemon juice, and while they cook, mix the arrowroot starch with the remaining water; pour the mixture into the berries. Stir and continue cooking the sauce to thicken to your desire. Turn off the heat and let it cool.

Finally, plate the crepes one on another and generously drizzle the raspberry sauce over them and serve.

Cheese & Prosciutto Frittata

Total Time: 25 minutes | Serves: 4

Per serving: Calories 347, Fat 30g; Net Carbs 1.9g; Protein 17.6g

Ingredients

10 slices prosciutto, chopped
10 fresh eggs
3 tbsp olive oil
½ cup almond milk

Salt and black pepper to taste
1½ cups mozzarella cheese
¼ cup chives, chopped

Directions

Grease a baking dish with cooking spray. Whisk the eggs, olive oil, almond milk, salt, and black pepper. Mix in the prosciutto and pour the mixture into the baking dish.

Sprinkle with mozzarella cheese and chives, and bake in the oven for 10 minutes at 400°F or until the eggs are thoroughly cooked. Cool frittata for 3 minutes, slice into wedges before and serve.

Carrot Zucchini Bread

Total Time: 70 minutes | Serves: 4

Per serving: Calories 224, Fat 15g; Net Carbs 5.1g; Protein 11.6g

Ingredients

3 carrots, shredded
⅓ cup almond flour
1 tsp vanilla extract
6 eggs
1 tbsp olive oil
¾ tsp baking soda

1 tbsp cinnamon powder
½ tsp salt
½ cup full-fat yogurt
1 tsp apple cider vinegar
½ tsp nutmeg powder

Directions

Grease the loaf pan with cooking spray. Set aside.

Mix the carrots, zucchinis, almond flour, vanilla extract, eggs, olive oil, baking soda, cinnamon powder, salt, yogurt, vinegar, and nutmeg. Pour the batter into the loaf pan and bake for 55 minutes at 350°F.

Remove the bread after and let cool for 5 minutes.

Pistachio & Mascarpone Pots

Total Time: 20 minutes | Serves: 4

Per serving: Calories 187; Fat: 13.5g; Net Carbs: 0.6g; Protein: 12.9g

Ingredients

½ cup Greek yogurt
10 oz mascarpone cheese
3 eggs, beaten
1 tbsp pistachios, ground

4 tbsp xylitol
½ tsp vanilla extract
⅓ tsp ground cinnamon

Directions

Grease a muffin pan with cooking spray. Mix all ingredients in a bowl. Split the batter into the muffin cups. Bake for 12 to 15 minutes at 360°F. Remove and set on a wire rack to cool slightly before serving.

Mozzarella & Chistorra Spanish Chorizo Omelet

Total Time: 15 minutes | Serves: 2

Per serving: Calories 451, Fat: 36.5g; Net Carbs: 3g; Protein: 30g

Ingredients

4 eggs
1 cup mozzarella cheese, shredded
1 tbsp olive oil
1 tbsp water

4 oz Chistorra Spanish Chorizo, sliced
2 tomatoes, sliced
Salt and black pepper, to taste

Directions

Whisk the eggs along with the water and some salt and pepper. Warm the olive oil in a skillet and cook the eggs for 30 seconds. Spread the chorizo slices over. Arrange the sliced tomato and mozzarella over the chorizo. Cook for about 3 minutes. Cover the skillet and continue cooking for 3 minutes until omelet is set.

When ready, remove the pan from heat; run a spatula around the edges of the omelet and flip it onto a warm plate, folded side down. Serve with green salad.

Morning Buttered Eggs

Total Time: 15 minutes | Serves: 2

Per serving: Calories 241, Fat: 21.5g; Net Carbs: 0.7g; Protein: 11.3g

Ingredients

1 tbsp olive oil
1 tbsp butter
1 tsp fresh rosemary
4 eggs

1 garlic clove, minced
½ cup parsley, chopped
¼ tsp cayenne pepper
Salt and black pepper, to taste

Directions

Warm olive oil in a skillet over medium heat. Add the butter, garlic and rosemary and cook for 30 seconds. Sprinkle with parsley. Crack the eggs into the skillet.

Lower the heat and cook for 4-6 minutes. Adjust the seasoning. When the eggs are just set, turn the heat off and transfer to a serving plate. Sprinkle with cayenne pepper and serve.

Nut Granola with Yogurt Smoothie

Total Time: 5 minutes | Serves: 4

Per serving: Calories 615, Fat 40.5g; Net Carbs 3.5g; Protein 29.8g

Ingredients

4 cups natural yogurt
4 tbsp peanut butter
A handful toasted walnuts
3 tbsp unsweetened almond powder
4 tsp swerve brown sugar

2 cups mixed raw nuts (of your choice)
1 tsp vanilla extract
1 tsp ground cinnamon
Salt to taste
2 tbsp olive oil

Directions

Preheat the oven to 320°F. In a baking dish, combine raw nuts, vanilla extract, cinnamon, salt, and olive oil, and mix well. Bake for 20 minutes. Remove from the oven and cool completely. Break into small pieces.

Combine the yogurt, peanut butter, walnuts, almond powder, and swerve brown sugar in a smoothie maker; puree until smooth and well mixed. Share the smoothie into bowls, top with granola, and serve.

Smoked Salmon & Mascarpone Omelet Roll

Total Time: 15 minutes | Serves: 3

Per serving: Calories 383, Fat: 33g; Net Carbs: 1.3g; Protein: 16.4g

Ingredients

1 avocado, sliced
3 spring onions, chopped
3 slices smoked salmon
3 eggs

2 tbsp mascarpone, at room temperature
2 tbsp olive oil
Salt and black pepper, to taste

Directions

In a bowl, beat the eggs and season with salt and black pepper. Warm olive oil over medium heat. Add in the eggs and cook for 3 minutes. Flip the omelet over and continue cooking for another 2 minutes until golden. Remove to a plate and spread the mascarpone, salmon, avocado, and chopped onions. Wrap the omelet and serve immediately.

Egg & Aioli Salad

Total Time: 20 minutes | Serves: 6

Per serving: Calories: 407; Fat 24g; Net Carbs 3.4g; Protein 35.9g

Ingredients

28 oz tuna in brine, drained
8 eggs
½ head Iceberg lettuce, torn
½ cup chives, chopped
½ cup ricotta cheese, crumbled
⅓ cup sour cream

½ tbsp mustard
1 cup mayonnaise
2 cloves garlic, minced
Juice of 1 lemon
Salt, to taste

Directions

Boil the eggs in salted water for 10 minutes over medium heat, remove to a bowl with ice cold water to cool, and then peel and chop in small pieces.

Mix the eggs with tuna, chives, mustard, ricotta cheese, Iceberg lettuce, and sour cream. In a separate bowl, combine mayonnaise, lemon juice, salt, and garlic.

Add the aioli to the egg mixture, stir well and serve in a serving platter.

Breakfast Almond Milk Shake

Total Time: 4 minutes | Serves: 2

Per serving: Calories 326, Fat: 27g; Net Carbs: 6g; Protein: 19g

Ingredients

3 cups almond milk
4 tbsp heavy cream
½ tsp vanilla extract
4 tbsp flax meal

2 tbsp protein powder
4 drops of liquid stevia
Ice cubes to serve

Directions

In the bowl of your food processor, add almond milk, heavy cream, flax meal, vanilla extract, collagen peptides, and stevia. Blitz until uniform and smooth, for about 30 seconds. Add a bit more almond milk if it's very thick. Pour in a smoothie glass, add the ice cubes and sprinkle with cinnamon.

Zucchini Patties with Pancetta

Total Time: 20 minutes | Serves: 3

Per serving: Calories 412, Fat: 29.7g, Net Carbs: 5.1g, Protein: 27.8g

Ingredients

3 medium zucchini, diced
6 slices pancetta
6 eggs
1 tbsp olive oil
1 small onion, chopped
1 tbsp parsley, chopped
Salt to taste

Directions

Cook the pancetta in a skillet over medium heat for 3-5 minutes, until crispy; set aside.

Warm the olive oil and cook the onion until soft, for 3 minutes, occasionally stirring. Add the zucchinis, and cook for 8 more minutes until zucchini is brown and tender, but not mushy. Transfer to a plate and season with salt.

Crack the egg into the same skillet and fry over medium heat. Top the zucchini mixture with the bacon slices and a fried egg. Serve hot, sprinkled with parsley.

Mozzarella & Broccoli Scramble

Total Time: 20 minutes | Serves: 4

Per serving: Calories 248; Fat: 17.1g; Net Carbs: 6.2g; Protein: 17.6g

Ingredients

2 tbsp olive oil
1 onion, chopped
1 small head broccoli, chopped
8 eggs, beaten
Salt and red pepper, to taste
¾ cup mozzarella cheese, grated
¼ cup fresh parsley, to serve

Directions

Sauté onion in a frying pan over medium heat until caramelized. Place in the broccoli and cook until tender. Add in mozzarella and eggs; season with red pepper and salt. Cook for 4-5 minutes, stirring frequently until the eggs are set.

Decorate with fresh parsley before serving.

LUNCH RECIPES

Lettuce & Radicchio Tuna Salad

Total Time: 5 minutes | Serves: 2

Per serving: Calories 248, Fat: 20g; Net Carbs: 2g; Protein: 18.5g

Ingredients

- 8 oz canned tuna, drained
- 1 tsp onion flakes
- 3 tbsp mayonnaise
- ½ small head Iceberg lettuce, shredded
- ½ head radicchio, sliced
- 1 tbsp lemon juice
- Sea salt to taste
- 6 black olives, pitted and sliced

Directions

In a salad platter, arrange shredded lettuce sliced radicchio, tuna, and onion flakes. Season with salt.

In a bowl, combine mayonnaise, lemon juice, and salt. Spread the mayonnaise mixture over the salad and top with black olives to serve.

Mediterranean Salad

Total Time: 10 minutes | Serves: 4

Per serving: Calories 290, Fat: 25g; Net Carbs: 4.3g; Protein: 9g

Ingredients

- ¼ lb feta cheese, sliced
- 3 tomatoes, sliced
- 1 large avocado, sliced
- 8 kalamata olives
- 2 tbsp pesto sauce
- 2 tbsp olive oil

Directions

On a serving platter, arrange the tomato slices and place the avocado slices in the middle. Arrange the olives around the avocado slices and drop pieces of feta on the platter. Drizzle the pesto sauce all over, and drizzle olive oil as well.

Baked Italian Sausage with Cheese Topping

Total Time: 25 minutes | Serves: 5

Per serving: Calories 582, Fat 42.8g; Net Carbs 8.2g; Protein 33g

Ingredients

3 tbsp olive oil
16 oz Italian pork sausage, chopped
8 oz mozzarella cheese, grated
1 onion, sliced
4 sun-dried tomatoes, sliced thin

Salt and black pepper, to taste
3 green bell peppers, seeded and chopped
2 orange bell peppers, seeded and chopped
A pinch of red pepper flakes
2 tbsp fresh parsley, chopped

Directions

Preheat oven to 340°F.

Warm olive oil in a pan over medium heat and cook the sausage slices, for 3 minutes on each side, remove to a bowl, and set aside.

Stir in the tomatoes, bell peppers, and onion, and cook for 5 minutes. Season with pepper, pepper flakes, and salt and mix well. Cook for 1 minute, and remove from heat.

Lay the sausage slices into a baking dish, place the bell peppers mixture on top, scatter with the mozzarella cheese and bake for 10 minutes until the cheese melts. Serve topped with parsley.

Butternut Squash Stuffed with Beef & Mushrooms

Total Time: 60 minutes | Serves: 4

Per serving: Calories 406, Fat 14.7g; Net Carbs 12.4g; Protein 34g

Ingredients

1 lb ground beef
2 tbsp olive oil
2 lb butternut squash, pricked with a fork
Salt and black pepper, to taste
3 garlic cloves, minced
2 green onions, chopped

1 portobello mushrooms, sliced
28 oz canned tomatoes
¼ tsp cayenne pepper
½ tsp dried thyme
½ lb green beans, halved crosswise

Directions

Bake the butternut squash on a lined baking sheet in the oven at 400°F for 40 minutes. Cut in half, set aside to let cool, deseed, scoop out most of the flesh and let sit.

Heat olive oil in a pan over medium heat, add in the garlic, mushrooms, green onions, and beef, and cook until the meat browns, about 6-8 minutes.

Stir in the green beans, salt, thyme, tomatoes, oregano, black pepper, and cayenne, and cook for 10 minutes; stir in the flesh.

Stuff the squash halves with the beef mixture, and bake in the oven for 10 minutes.

Chicken Lettuce Wraps

Total Time: 20 minutes | Serves: 4

Per serving: Calories 325, Fat 24.5g; Net Carbs 4g; Protein 21g

Ingredients

8 romaine lettuce leaves
1 pound chicken breasts, cubed
1 tbsp olive oil
Salt and black pepper to taste

6 large eggs
1½ cups water
2 tomatoes, seeded and chopped
6 tbsp natural yogurt

Directions

Coat the chicken cubes with olive oil, salt, and black pepper. Spread out evenly on a greased baking dish and slide in the oven.

Bake the chicken in the oven at 400°F until cooked through and golden brown for 8 minutes, turning once.

Bring the eggs to boil in salted water in a pot over medium heat for 10 minutes. Run the eggs in cold water, peel, and chop into small pieces. Transfer to a bowl.

Remove the chicken from the oven, let cool for a few minutes and add to the eggs. Include the tomatoes and yogurt; mix well.

Layer two lettuce leaves each as cups and fill with two tablespoons of egg mixture each. Serve with chilled blueberry juice.

Prawn & Arugula Salad

Total Time: 15 minutes | Serves: 4

Per serving: Calories 215, Fat 20.3g; Net Carbs 2g; Protein 8g

Ingredients

32 oz arugula
4 oz mayonnaise
1 garlic clove, minced
2 tbsp olive oil

1 lb tiger prawns, peeled and deveined
1 tsp Dijon mustard
Salt and chili pepper to taste
Juice of 1 lemon

Directions

Mix the mayonnaise, garlic, lemon juice and mustard in a small bowl until smooth.

Heat olive oil in a skillet over medium heat, add the prawns, season with salt and chili pepper, and fry in the oil for 3 minutes on each side until prawns are pink; set aside.

Place the arugula in a serving bowl and pour half of the dressing on the top. Toss until mixed, and add the remaining dressing. Divide salad onto plates and top with prawns.

Roasted Pork with Green Sauce

Total Time: 40 minutes | Serves: 4

Per serving: Calories 430, Fat 23g; Net Carbs 3g; Protein 45g

Ingredients

1 pound pork loin
2 tbsp olive oil
Salt and black pepper, to taste
¼ tsp dry mustard
1 tsp hot red pepper flakes

16 oz kale, chopped
2 garlic cloves, minced
½ lemon sliced
¼ cup water

Directions

Place the pork in a bowl and toss with salt, mustard, and black pepper to coat. Heat the oil in a saucepan over medium heat, brown the pork on all sides, for 10 minutes.

Transfer to the oven and roast for 1 hour at 390°F. To the saucepan, add kale, lemon slices, garlic, and water; cook for 10 minutes. Serve on a platter and sprinkle pan juices on top.

Vegetable Frittata

Total Time: 25 minutes | Serves: 4

Per serving: Calories 310; Fat: 26.2g; Net Carbs: 3.9g; Protein: 15.4g

Ingredients

2 tbsp olive oil
½ cup green onions, chopped
2 garlic cloves, minced
1 jalapeño pepper, chopped
1 carrot, chopped
1 zucchini, chopped
1 bell pepper, seeded and chopped
8 eggs
Salt and black pepper, to taste
½ tsp dried thyme

Directions

Preheat the oven to 350°F.

Warm olive oil in a pan over medium heat. Stir in green onions and garlic, and sauté for 3 minutes until tender. Pour in carrot, zucchini, bell pepper, and jalapeño pepper, and cook for 4 minutes. Remove the mixture to a greased baking pan with cooking spray.

In a bowl, whisk the eggs, season with salt and pepper, and pour over vegetables. Bake for about 18 minutes.

Anchovy Caprese Salad

Total Time: 10 minutes | Serves: 4

Per serving: Calories 360, Fat 31g; Net Carbs 1g; Protein 21g

Ingredients

4 tomatoes, sliced
6 anchovy fillets in oil
10 oz Buffalo mozzarella cheese, sliced
1 bunch of basil leaves
2 tbsp extra virgin olive oil
2 tsp balsamic vinegar

Directions

Alternate a slice of tomato, cheese, and a basil leaf in a serving platter.

Cut the anchovies lengthwise in two. Arrange them over the tomato and mozzarella slices. To finish, drizzle with olive oil and balsamic vinegar and serve.

Minty Pesto Rubbed Pork Chops

Total Time: 3 hours 10 minutes | Serves: 4

Per serving: Calories 758, Fat 63.8g; Net Carbs 1.5g; Protein 37g

Ingredients

1 cup mint
1 onion, chopped
⅓ cup hazelnuts
1½ pounds pork chops
1 lemon zested and juiced
5 tbsp olive oil
Salt to taste
3 garlic cloves, minced

Directions

Preheat oven to 250°F.

In a food processor, combine the parsley with olive oil, mint, hazelnuts, salt, lemon zest, and onion. Rub the pork with this mixture, place in a bowl, and refrigerate for 1 hour while covered. Remove the chops and set to a baking dish, place in garlic, sprinkle with lemon juice, and bake in the oven for 2 hours.

Juicy Pork Chops with Olives

Total Time: 45 minutes | Serves: 4

Per serving: Calories 631, Fat 51.2g; Net Carbs 0.1g; Protein 38.8g

Ingredients

1½ pounds pork chops, bone-in
¼ cup chicken broth
Salt and black pepper, to taste
1 tsp dried oregano
3 garlic cloves, minced
½ cup kalamata olives, pitted and sliced
2 tbsp olive oil

Directions

Preheat oven to 425°F.

Place the pork in a baking pan and season pork chops with pepper and salt. Stir in the garlic, olives, olive oil, broth, and rosemary, and bake in the oven for 10 minutes. Reduce heat to 350°F and roast for 25 minutes. Slice the pork, split among plates, and sprinkle with pan juices all over.

Ground Beef with Cauliflower and Cabbage in Oven

Total Time: 30 minutes | Serves: 6

Per serving: Calories 385, Fat 25g; Net Carbs 5g; Protein 20g

Ingredients

2 pounds ground beef
Salt and black pepper to taste
1 cup riced cauliflower
1 head cabbage, shredded
14 oz can diced tomatoes
1 cup shredded cheese

Directions

Grease a baking dish with cooking spray. Put beef in a pot and season with salt and black pepper and cook over medium heat for 6 minutes until no longer pink. Drain the grease. Add cauli rice, cabbage, tomatoes, and ¼ cup of water. Stir and bring to boil covered for 5 minutes to thicken the sauce. Adjust taste with salt and black pepper.

Preheat oven to 370°F. Spoon the beef mixture into the baking dish and spread evenly. Sprinkle with cheese and bake for 15 minutes until cheese has melted and it's golden brown. Remove and cool for 4 minutes before serving.

Oregano Tomato Cream Soup

Total Time: 20 minutes | Serves: 5

Per serving: Calories 310, Fat 27g; Net Carbs 3g; Protein 11g

Ingredients

2 tbsp olive oil
2 large red onions, diced
½ cup raw macadamia nuts
28 oz canned tomatoes
1 tsp oregano leaves + extra to garnish
4 cups vegetable stock
Salt and black pepper to taste
1 cup heavy cream

Directions

Warm olive oil in a pot over medium heat and sauté the onions for 3 minutes until softened. Stir in the tomatoes, oregano, vegetable stock, macadamia, and season with salt and black pepper. Cover and bring to simmer for 10 minutes until thoroughly cooked.

Puree the ingredients with an immersion blender. Adjust to taste and stir in the heavy cream and serve.

Homemade Rolled Porchetta Roast with Pine Nuts

Total Time: 60 minutes | Serves: 4

Per serving: Calories 581, Fat 48.3g; Net Carbs 1.3g; Protein 32g

Ingredients

1 lb rolled pork shoulder, boneless
2 tbsp fresh sage, chopped
3 tbsp fennel seeds
1 cup pine nuts
3 cloves garlic, minced
Salt and black pepper to taste

Directions

In a bowl, combine the fresh sage, fennel seeds, pine nuts, and garlic. Season with salt and black pepper. Untie the pork flat onto a chopping board, spread the sage mixture all over, and rub the spice into the meat. Roll the pork over the spice mixture and tie it together using 3 to 4 strings of butcher's twine.

Place the pork onto a greased with cooking spray baking dish and cook in the oven for 10 minutes at 450°F. Reduce the heat to 350°F and continue cooking for 40 minutes. When ready, transfer the meat to a cleaned chopping board; let it rest for 10 minutes before slicing.

Pork Sausage & Pancetta with Kale

Total Time: 30 minutes | Serves: 6

Per serving: Calories 356, Fat 29g; Net Carbs 5.4g; Protein 21g

Ingredients

8 cups chicken broth
1 tbsp olive oil
1 cup heavy cream
16 oz kale
4 oz pancetta, chopped
2 garlic cloves, minced
Salt and black pepper, to taste
A pinch of red pepper flakes
1 onion, chopped
8 pork sausage, chopped

Directions

Warm oil in a pot over medium heat. Stir in garlic, onion, pancetta, and sausage; cook for 5 minutes. Pour in broth and kale, and simmer for 10 minutes. Stir in the salt, red pepper flakes, pepper, and heavy cream, and cook for about 5 minutes. Split among serving bowls and enjoy the meal.

Summer Spanish Gazpacho with Ricotta Cheese

Total Time: 15 minutes | Serves: 4

Per serving: Calories 617, Fat: 54.5g; Net Carbs: 6.5g; Protein: 9.9g

Ingredients

6 oz ricotta cheese
2 green bell peppers
2 red bell peppers
2 garlic cloves
2 red onions, chopped
1 cucumber, chopped
1 cup extra virgin olive oil
Juice of 1 lemon
6 tomatoes, chopped
3 cups tomato juice
2 tbsp apple cider vinegar
Salt to taste

Directions

In a blender, put the bell peppers, tomatoes, tomato juice, cucumber, red onion, garlic, lemon juice, olive oil, vinegar, and salt. Pulse until your desired consistency is reached. Taste and adjust the seasoning.

Cover and chill in the fridge at least 2 hours. Divide between serving bowls. Serve topped with goat cheese and an extra drizzle of extra virgin olive oil.

Classic Greek Salad

Total Time: 10 minutes | Serves: 4

Per serving: Calories 323, Fat: 28g; Net Carbs: 8g; Protein: 9.3g

Ingredients

1 red bell pepper, roasted and chopped
5 tomatoes, chopped
1 large cucumber, chopped
1 small red onion, sliced
16 kalamata olives, chopped
1 cup feta cheese, cubed
1 tsp oregano, dried
4 tbsp olive oil
Juice of 1 lemon
Salt to taste

Directions

Place tomatoes, roasted bell pepper, cucumber, onion, feta cheese and olives in a bowl; mix to combine well. Season with salt. Combine lemon juice, olive oil, and oregano, in a small bowl. Drizzle with the dressing to serve.

Caesar Salad with Smoked Salmon and Poached Eggs

Total Time: 15 minutes | Serves: 4

Per serving: Calories 260, Fat 21g; Net Carbs 5g; Protein 8g

Ingredients

3 cups water
8 eggs
2 cups torn romaine lettuce
½ cup chopped smoked salmon
6 slices bacon
2 tbsp low carb Caesar dressing

Directions

Boil the water in a pot over medium heat for 5 minutes and bring to simmer. Crack each egg into a small bowl and gently slide into the water. Poach for 2 to 3 minutes, remove with a perforated spoon, transfer to a paper towel to dry, and plate. Poach the remaining 7 eggs.

Put the bacon in a skillet and fry over medium heat until browned and crispy, about 6 minutes, turning once. Remove, allow cooling, and chop in small pieces.

Toss the lettuce, smoked salmon, bacon, and Caesar dressing in a salad bowl. Divide the salad into 4 plates, top with two eggs each, and serve immediately or chilled.

Greek Moussaka

Total Time: 45 minutes | Serves: 4

Per serving: Calories 454, Fat 17.8g; Net Carbs 9.9g; Protein 53.4g

Ingredients

1½ pounds ground beef
1 onion, chopped
2 eggplants, sliced
3 cloves garlic
15 oz canned tomatoes, chopped
Salt and black pepper to taste
2 tsp paprika
1 tbsp fresh parsley, chopped
4 oz mozzarella cheese, shredded
1 cup natural yogurt
1 egg, beaten
1 tbsp olive oil

Directions

Lightly grease a baking dish with cooking spray. Lay the eggplant slices on a paper towel and sprinkle with salt; set aside.

Warm the olive oil in a skillet and cook the ground beef for 4 minutes while breaking any lumps as you stir. Top with onion, garlic, tomatoes, salt, paprika, and pepper. Stir and continue cooking for 5 minutes.

Back to the eggplants, use a paper towel to blot out any liquid on it and lay ⅓ of the slices in the baking dish. Top with ⅓ of the beef mixture and repeat the layering process two more times with the same quantities.

In a small bowl, mix the yogurt with egg; season with salt and black pepper. Spread this mixture on top and tuck the baking dish in the oven. Bake for 15 minutes at 370°F.

Remove the moussaka and sprinkle with the mozzarella cheese and return to the oven. Bake for 5-10 minutes until the golden brown. Serve the moussaka garnished with parsley.

Mixed Grilled Vegetables with Beef Steaks

Total Time: 30 minutes | Serves: 4

Per serving: Calories 515, Fat 32.1g; Net Carbs 5.6g; Protein 66g

Ingredients

1 pound sirloin steaks
4 tbsp olive oil
Vegetables
4 asparagus, trimmed
1 red onion, quartered
1 cup green beans

Salt and black pepper to taste
3 tbsp balsamic vinegar

1 cup snow peas
1 red bell peppers, seeded, cut into strips
1 green bell peppers, seeded, cut into strips

Directions

Grab 2 separate bowls; put the beef in one and the vegetables in another. Mix salt, black pepper, olive oil, and balsamic vinegar in a small bowl, and pour half of the mixture over the beef and the other half over the vegetables. Coat the ingredients in both bowls with the sauce.

Place the steaks in the grill pan over high heat, and sear both sides for 2 minutes each, then continue cooking for 6 minutes on each side. When done, remove the beef to a plate; set aside.

Pour the vegetables and marinade in the same grill pan; and cook for 5 minutes, turning once. Turn the heat off and share the vegetables into four plates. Top with each piece of beef, the sauce from the pan, and serve.

Gorgonzola & Pancetta Green Salad

Total Time: 15 minutes | Serves: 3

Per serving: Calories 205, Fat 20g; Net Carbs 2g; Protein 4g

Ingredients

3 cups salad greens
6 pancetta slices
1 cup gorgonzola cheese, crumbled
1 tbsp white wine vinegar
3 tbsp extra virgin olive oil
Salt and black pepper to taste

Directions

Place the salad greens in a bowl; set aside. In a skillet over medium heat, fry pancetta slices for 6 minutes, until crispy. Chop pancetta and scatter over the salad. Add in half of the gorgonzola, toss and set aside.

In a small bowl, whisk the white wine vinegar, olive oil, salt, and black pepper until dressing is well combined. Drizzle half of the dressing over the salad, toss, and top with remaining gorgonzola cheese. Divide salad into four plates and serve with crusted chicken fries along with remaining dressing.

Tasty Dijon Pork Chops

Total Time: 2 hours 20 minutes | Serves: 6

Per serving: Calories 418, Fat 26.8g; Net Carbs 1.5g; Protein 38.1g

Ingredients

1½ pounds pork loin chops, boneless
2 tbsp xylitol
3 tbsp Dijon mustard
3 cloves garlic, minced
¼ cup olive oil
Salt and black pepper to taste

Directions

Put the pork in a plastic bag. In a bowl, mix the xylitol, mustard, garlic, olive oil, salt, pepper, and pour the sauce over the pork. Seal the bag, shake it, and place in the refrigerator. Marinate the pork for 1 to 2 hours.

Preheat the grill on medium-high heat, remove the pork when ready, and grill covered for 10 to 12 minutes on each side. Remove the pork chops, let sit for 4 minutes, and serve.

Easy Green Soup

Total Time: 25 minutes | Serves: 5

Per serving: Calories 392, Fat: 37.6g; Net Carbs: 5.8g; Protein: 4.9g

Ingredients

1 broccoli head, chopped
1 cup kale, chopped
2 spring onions, chopped
2 garlic cloves, minced
½ cup green cabbage, shredded
4 cups water
1 cup almond milk
1 tbsp olive oil
Salt and black pepper, to taste
2 tbsp fresh basil, chopped

Directions

Warm olive oil in a large pot over medium heat. Add onion and garlic, and cook for 3 minutes until tender. Add broccoli and green cabbage and cook for an additional 10 minutes. Pour water over and bring to a boil; reduce the heat. Simmer for about 3 minutes.

In the end, add kale and cook for 3 more minutes. Stir in the almond milk, salt and pepper. Blend the soup with a hand blender. Serve topped with chopped fresh basil.

Dilled Baby Artichoke Salad

Total Time: 30 minutes | Serves: 4

Per serving: Calories 170, Fat: 13g; Net Carbs: 5g; Protein: 1g

Ingredients

1 lb baby artichokes, halved
6 cups water
Juice and zest of 1 lemon
¼ cup piquillo peppers, chopped
¼ cup olives, pitted and sliced
¼ cup olive oil
2 tsp balsamic vinegar, sugar-free
1 tbsp dill, chopped
Salt and black pepper to taste
1 tbsp capers

Directions

Add the artichokes to a filled with salted water. Bring to a boil, lower the heat, and let simmer for 20 minutes until tender. Combine the rest of the ingredients, except the olives in a bowl. Drain and place the artichokes in a serving plate. Pour the prepared mixture over; toss to combine well. Serve topped with the olives.

Veggie and Pork Osso Bucco

Total Time: 1 hour 55 minutes | Serves: 4

Per serving: Calories 616, Fat 40g; Net Carbs 4.1g; Protein 34g

Ingredients

4 tbsp olive oil
½ onion, chopped
½ stalk celery, chopped
1 carrot, chopped
1 pound pork shanks
3 cloves garlic, minced

1 cup diced tomatoes
Salt and black pepper to taste
16 oz Merlot
5 cups vegetable broth
½ cup chopped parsley + extra to garnish
2 tsp lemon zest

Directions

Warm the olive oil in a large saucepan over medium heat and brown the pork for 12 minutes. Season with salt and pepper and remove to a plate.

In the same pan, sauté 2 cloves of garlic and onion, for 3 minutes then return the pork shanks. Stir in the Merlot, carrots, celery, tomatoes, and vegetable broth. Cover the pan and let it simmer on low heat for 1½ hours basting the pork every 15 minutes with the sauce.

In a bowl, mix the remaining garlic, parsley, and lemon zest to make a gremolata, and stir the mixture into the sauce when it is ready. Turn the heat off and dish the osso bucco. Garnish with parsley and serve.

Cauliflower Cream Soup with Pancetta & Chives

Total Time: 25 minutes | Serves: 4

Per serving: Calories 663, Fat 60g; Net Carbs 9.7g; Protein 18g

Ingredients

2 tbsp olive oil
1 leek, chopped
2 head cauliflower, cut into florets
2 cups vegetable broth
Salt and black pepper to taste

3 cups almond milk
1 cup mozzarella cheese, shredded
4 pancetta slices
1 tbsp chives, chopped

Directions

In a saucepan over high heat, fry the pancetta, until crispy; set aside. To the same saucepan add olive oil and sauté the onion for 3 minutes until fragrant.

Pour in the cauli florets, sauté for 3 minutes to slightly soften, add the vegetable broth, and season with salt and black pepper. Bring to a boil, and then reduce the heat to low. Cover and cook for 10 minutes.

Puree cauliflower with an immersion blender until the ingredients are evenly combined and stir in the almond milk and cheese until the cheese melts. Adjust taste with salt and black pepper.

Divide soup between serving bowls, top with crispy pancetta and chives, and serve hot.

Balsamic Glazed Beef Meatloaf

Total Time: 55 minutes | Serves: 8

Per serving: Calories 294, Fat: 19g; Net Carbs: 6g; Protein: 23g

Ingredients

2 pounds ground beef
4 tbsp almond flour
2 small onions, chopped
2 garlic cloves, minced
3 eggs
Glaze:
1 drop liquid stevia

Salt and black pepper to taste
2 tbsp parsley, chopped
2 bell peppers, chopped
3 tbsp Parmesan cheese, grated

1 cup balsamic vinegar

Directions

Preheat the oven to 370°F. Combine all meatloaf ingredients in a large bowl. Press this mixture into a greased loaf pan. Bake for about 30 minutes.

Make the glaze by combining stevia and balsamic vinegar in a saucepan over medium heat. Simmer for 5-10 minutes, or until the glaze is thickened. Pour the glaze over the meatloaf. Put the meatloaf back in the oven and cook for 10 more minutes.

Turkey Pizza with Pesto Topping

Total Time: 35 minutes | Serves: 5

Per serving: Calories 684, Fat 54g; Net Carbs 2g; Protein 31.5g

Ingredients

Pizza Bread

3 cups almond flour
3 tbsp olive oil
⅓ tsp salt
3 large eggs

Pesto Chicken Topping

½ pound turkey ham, chopped
2 tbsp cashew nuts
Salt and black pepper to taste
1½ tbsp olive oil
1 green bell pepper, seeded and sliced
1½ cups basil pesto
1 cup mozzarella cheese, grated
1½ tbsp Parmesan cheese, grated
1½ tbsp fresh basil leaves
A pinch of red pepper flakes

Directions

In a bowl, mix almond flour, 3 tbsp of olive oil, salt, and eggs until a dough forms. Mold the dough into a ball and place it in between two full parchment papers on a flat surface.

Roll it out into a circle of a ¼-inch thickness. After, slide the pizza dough into the pizza pan and remove the parchment paper. Place the pizza pan in the oven and bake the dough for 20 minutes at 350°F.

Once the pizza bread is ready, remove it from the oven, fold and seal the extra inch of dough at its edges to make a crust around it. Apply 2/3 of the pesto on it and sprinkle half of the mozzarella cheese too. Toss the chopped turkey ham in the remaining pesto and spread it on top of the pizza.

Sprinkle with the remaining mozzarella, bell peppers, and cashew nuts and put the pizza back in the oven to bake for 9 minutes.

When it is ready, remove from the oven to cool slightly, garnish with the basil leaves and sprinkle with parmesan cheese and red pepper flakes. Slice and serve with green salad.

Zucchini Frittata with Tomato & Bresaola Salad

Total Time: 56 minutes | Serves: 4

Per serving: Calories 366, Fat 31.5g; Net Carbs 5.2g; Protein 13g

Ingredients

1 cup mushrooms, sliced
8 eggs
2 tbsp almond milk
Salt and black pepper to taste

Chorizo and Tomato Salad

4 oz bresaola, thinly sliced
4 tomatoes, cut into wedges
1 small red onion, thinly sliced

1 garlic clove, minced
2 tbsp olive oil
1 cup zucchini, shredded
¼ cup mozzarella cheese, grated

1 tbsp plain vinegar
2 sprigs thyme, leaves picked
2 tbsp olive oil

Directions

Grease a baking dish with cooking spray.

Heat 1 tbsp of olive oil in a skillet over medium heat and stir-fry the mushrooms to sweat for about 4 minutes. Add the minced garlic, salt, and pepper. Sauté for 30 seconds to make the garlic fragrant.

Stir in zucchini and cook for 5 minutes. Increase the heat and let the excess liquid evaporate. Adjust the taste with salt and pepper.

Beat the eggs in a large bowl and stir in almond milk, salt, pepper, the mushroom mixture, and mozzarella cheese. Pour the mixture into the baking dish and bake in the oven for 25 minutes at 350°F.

In a salad bowl, add the tomatoes, onion, bresaola, and thyme. Drizzle the vinegar and a little oil over them, and toss the ingredients. Slice the frittata into wedges. Serve warm with the salad.

Broccoli Cheese Soup

Total Time: 20 minutes | Serves: 4

Per serving: Calories 561, Fat: 52.3g; Net Carbs: 7g; Protein: 23.8g

Ingredients

¾ cup heavy cream
1 onion, diced
1 tsp minced garlic
4 cups chopped broccoli
4 cups veggie broth

2 tbsp butter
2 ¾ cups grated cheddar cheese
¼ cup cheddar cheese to garnish
Salt and black pepper, to taste
½ bunch fresh mint, chopped

Directions

Melt the butter in a large pot over medium heat. Sauté onion and garlic for 3 minutes or until tender, stirring occasionally. Season with salt and pepper. Add the broth, broccoli and bring to a boil.

Reduce the heat and simmer for 10 minutes. Puree the soup with a hand blender until smooth. Add in the cheese and cook about 1 minute. Taste, season with salt and pepper. Stir in the heavy cream. Serve in bowls with the reserved grated Cheddar cheese and sprinkled with fresh mint.

Baked Pork Sausages

Total Time: 35 minutes | Serves: 4

Per serving: Calories 465, Fat 41.6g; Net Carbs 4.4g; Protein 15.1g

Ingredients

1 pound pork sausages
3 bell peppers, in different colors, sliced
4 large tomatoes, cut in rings
1 sprig thyme, chopped
1 sprig rosemary, chopped

2 cloves garlic, minced
2 bay leaves
1 tbsp olive oil
2 tbsp balsamic vinegar

Directions

In the cast iron pan, add the tomatoes, bell peppers, thyme, rosemary, garlic, bay leaves, sausages, olive oil, and balsamic vinegar. Toss everything and arrange the sausages on top of the veggies.

Put the pan in the oven and bake for 20 minutes at 350°F. After, remove the pan shake it a bit and turn the sausages over with a spoon. Continue cooking them for 10 minutes or until the sausages have browned to your desired color. Serve with the veggie and cooking sauce with cauli rice.

Parsley Beef Meatballs with Marinara Sauce

Total Time: 45 minutes | Serves: 6

Per serving: Calories 775, Fat 41g; Net Carbs 9.8g; Protein 76.3g

Ingredients

1½ pounds ground beef
1 tbsp olive oil
1 cup pork rinds, crushed
2 cloves garlic, minced
½ cup almond milk

1 egg, beaten
½ cup Parmesan cheese, grated
Salt and black pepper to taste
6 cups marinara sauce, sugar-free
Chopped parsley to garnish

Directions

Line a baking pan with foil and oil it with cooking spray. Set aside.

Combine the almond milk and pork rinds in a bowl. Mix in the ground beef, garlic, Parmesan cheese, egg, salt, and black pepper, until combined. Form balls of the mixture and place them in the prepared pan.

Preheat the oven to 350°F. Bake the meatballs for 20 minutes. Pour the marinara sauce in a saucepan and bring to a simmer, stirring occasionally, about 10 minutes.

Arrange the meatballs on a platter and spoon the marinara sauce on top. Sprinkle with chopped parsley to serve.

Fried Cod with White Wine Sauce

Total Time: 20 minutes | Serves: 6

Per serving: Calories 264, Fat 17.3g; Net Carbs 2.3g; Protein 20g

Ingredients

4 tsp olive oil
1½ pound cod fillets
4 garlic cloves, minced
Juice of 1 lemon
3 tbsp white wine
2 green onions, chopped
Salt and black pepper to taste

Directions

Heat 2 tbsp of the oil in a skillet over medium heat and season the cod with salt and black pepper. Fry the fillets in the oil for 4 minutes on one side, flip and cook for 1 minute. Take out, plate, and set aside.

In another skillet over low heat, warm the remaining olive oil and sauté the garlic for 3 minutes. Add the lemon juice, white wine, and green onions. Season with salt, black pepper, and cook for 3 minutes until the wine slightly reduces.

Put the fish in the skillet, spoon sauce over, cook for 30 seconds and turn the heat off. Divide fish into plates, top with sauce, and serve with steamed green beans.

Feta & Zucchini Gratin

Total Time: 65 minutes | Serves: 6

Per serving: Calories 264, Fat 21g; Net Carbs 4g; Protein 14g

Ingredients

2 green bell peppers, seeded and sliced
4 zucchinis, sliced and squeezed
Salt and black pepper to taste
12 oz feta cheese, crumbled
⅓ cup mozzarella cheese for topping
2 tbsp olive oil
¼ tsp xanthan gum
½ cup heavy whipping cream

Directions

Grease a baking dish with cooking spray and make a layer of zucchini and bell peppers in the dish overlapping one on another.

Season with black pepper, and sprinkle with some feta cheese. Repeat the layering process a second time.

Combine the olive oil, xanthan gum, and whipping cream in a microwave dish for 2 minutes, stir to mix completely, and pour over the vegetables. Top with mozzarella cheese. Bake the gratin for 45 minutes to be golden brown on top. Cut out slices and serve with salad.

Anchovy Caesar Salad

Total Time: 1 hour and 30 minutes | Serves: 4

Per serving: Calories 529, Fat: 39g; Net Carbs: 5g; Protein: 33g

Ingredients

1 lb chicken breasts, boneless, sliced
Juice of 1 lemon
2 garlic cloves, minced
6 tbsp olive oil

2 anchovies, mashed
2 small bunches watercress, stems trimmed
2 oz Parmesan cheese, shaved

Directions

In a Ziploc bag, combine the, chicken, 2 tbsp of olive oil, and half of the garlic. Seal the bag, shake to combine, and refrigerate for 1 hour.

Preheat the grill to medium heat and grill the chicken for about 4 minutes per side. In a bowl, whisk the mashed anchovies, remaining olive oil and garlic, and lemon juice. Season with salt and black pepper.

Place the watercress in a serving platter, add in the shaved parmesan cheese and grilled chicken and pour the anchovy dressing over to serve.

Pancetta and Green Veggie Gratin

Total Time: 35 minutes | Serves: 4

Per serving: Calories 350, Fat 27g; Net Carbs 5.3g; Protein 16g

Ingredients

2 oz pancetta, chopped
2 zucchinis, chopped
32 oz spinach
4 oz halloumi cheese, cut into cubes
8 oz tomato sauce, sugar-free

2 cloves garlic, minced
16 oz heavy cream
1 cup mozzarella cheese, grated
½ tsp dried Italian mixed herbs
Salt and black pepper to taste

Directions

Place the cast iron pan over medium heat and fry the pancetta for 4 minutes, then add garlic and cook for 1 minute.

In a bowl, mix the heavy cream, tomato sauce, and 1 tbsp of water, and add it to the pan. Stir in the zucchini, spinach, halloumi, Italian herbs, salt, and pepper to taste.

Turn the heat off, sprinkle the mozzarella cheese on top, and transfer the pan to the oven. Bake for 20 minutes at or until the cheese is golden. When ready, remove the pan and serve the gratin warm.

Herby Salmon with Creamy Sauce

Total Time: 20 minutes | Serves: 2

Per serving: Calories 468, Fat: 40g; Net Carbs: 1.5g; Protein: 22g

Ingredients

½ pound salmon fillets
¾ tsp tarragon
1 tbsp olive oil
Sauce
2 tbsp olive oil
½ tsp dill

¾ tsp dill, chopped
Sea salt to taste

½ tsp tarragon
¼ cup heavy cream

Directions

Warm 1 tbsp of olive oil in a pan over medium heat. Season the salmon with sea salt, dill and tarragon. Cook in the hot oil for about 4 minutes on both sides. Set aside.

In the same pan, add the remaining olive oil, dill and tarragon. Cook for 30 seconds to infuse the flavors. Whisk in the heavy cream and cook for one more minute. Serve the salmon topped with the sauce.

Almond-Crusted Salmon

Total Time: 35 minutes | Serves: 4

Per serving: Calories 563, Fat: 47g; Net Carbs: 6g; Protein: 34g

Ingredients

1 pound salmon fillets
½ cup almonds, chopped
Sauce
1 red onion, chopped
Zest of ½ lemon
1 tbsp olive oil

Sea salt black pepper to taste
4 tbsp mayonnaise

A pinch of black pepper
1 cup heavy cream

Directions

Brush the salmon with mayonnaise and season with salt and pepper. Coat with almonds. Place in a lined baking dish and bake in the oven for 15 minutes at 370°F.

Heat the olive oil in a saucepan and sauté the shallot for 3 minutes. Stir in the rest of the sauce ingredients. Bring the mixture to a boil and cook until thickened. Serve the fish with the sauce.

Tuscan Salmon Salad

Total Time: 22 minutes | Serves: 4

Per serving: Calories 338, Fat 21.7g; Net Carbs 3.1g; Protein 28.5g

Ingredients

4 steaks skinned salmon
1 cucumber, peeled, seeded, cubed
Salt and black pepper to taste
½ cup black olives, pitted and chopped
1 tbsp capers, rinsed
2 large tomatoes, diced
3 tbsp red wine vinegar
1 red onion, sliced
3 tbsp olive oil
2 slices zero carb bread, cubed
¼ cup basil leaves, thinly sliced

Directions

In a bowl, mix the cucumbers, olives, black pepper, capers, tomatoes, wine vinegar, onion, olive oil, bread, and basil leaves. Let sit for the flavors to incorporate.

Season the salmon steaks with salt and pepper; grill them on both sides for 8 minutes in total. Serve the salmon steaks warm on a bed of the salad.

Baked Fish with Parmesan Topping

Total Time: 40 minutes | Serves: 4

Per serving: Calories 354, Fat 17g; Net Carbs 4g; Protein 28g

Ingredients

½ pound salmon fillets, cubed
Sea salt and black pepper to taste
½ pound cod, cubed
1 broccoli, cut into florets
1 tbsp olive oil
1 cup crème fraiche
¼ cup Parmesan cheese, grated
Parmesan cheese, grated for topping

Directions

Grease a baking dish with cooking spray. Toss the fish and broccoli in oil and season with salt and black pepper. Spread in the greased dish. Mix the crème fraiche with Parmesan cheese, pour and smear the cream on the fish, and sprinkle with some more Parmesan.

Bake for 25 to 30 minutes in the oven at 400°F until golden brown on top, take the dish out, sit for 5 minutes and spoon into plates.

SNACKS

Homemade Biscuits with Mascarpone Snap

Total Time: 25 minutes | Serves: 6

Per serving: Calories 165, Fat 13g; Net Carbs 3g; Protein 9g

Ingredients

7 tbsp hazelnut liquor, sugar-free
6 egg whites
1 egg yolk, beaten
1 tsp vanilla bean paste
8 oz swerve confectioner's sugar
¼ tsp salt
¼ cup fragrant hazelnuts, ground
Juice of 1 lemon
¼ cup mascarpone cheese
¼ cup butter, room temperature
¾ cup swerve confectioner's sugar, for topping

Directions

Line a baking sheet with parchment paper.

In a bowl, beat eggs whites, salt, and vanilla paste while you gradually spoon in 8 oz of swerve confectioner's sugar until a stiff mixture. Add hazelnuts and fold in the egg yolk, lemon juice, and hazelnut liquor. Spoon the mixture into the piping bag and press out 40 to 50 mounds on the baking sheet.

Bake the biscuits in the oven for 15 minutes at 300°F by which time they should be golden brown.

Whisk the mascarpone cheese, butter, and swerve confectioner's sugar set aside.

When the biscuits are ready, transfer them into a serving bowl and let cool. Spread a scoop of mascarpone cream onto one biscuit and snap with another biscuit. Sift some swerve confectioner's sugar on top of them and serve.

Chicken Fritters with Rosemary Dip

Total Time: 40 minutes + cooling time | Serves: 4

Per serving: Calories 151, Fat 7g; Net Carbs 0.8g; Protein 12g

Ingredients

4 tbsp rosemary, chopped
2 chicken breasts, thinly sliced
1 ¼ cup mayonnaise
¼ cup almond flour
2 eggs
Salt and black pepper to taste
1 cup mozzarella cheese, grated
3 tbsp olive oil
1 cup buttermilk
1 tsp garlic powder
1 tbsp parsley, chopped
½ onion, chopped

Directions

Mix the chicken, ¼ cup of mayonnaise, almond flour, eggs, salt, pepper, mozzarella, and 1 tbsp of rosemary, in a bowl. Cover the bowl with plastic wrap and refrigerate it for 2 hours. After the marinating time is over, remove from the fridge.

In a bowl, mix the remaining mayonnaise, remaining rosemary, buttermilk, garlic powder, onion, and salt. Cover the bowl with plastic wrap and refrigerate for 30 minutes.

Place a skillet over medium fire and heat the olive oil. Fetch 2 tablespoons of chicken mixture into the skillet, use the back of a spatula to flatten the top. Cook for 4 minutes, flip, and fry for 4 more.

Remove onto a wire rack and repeat the cooking process until the batter is finished, adding more oil as needed. Garnish the fritters with parsley and serve with rosemary dip.

Cheesy Crackers

Total Time: 25 minutes | Serves: 6

Per serving: Calories 115, Fat 3g; Net Carbs 0.7g; Protein 5g

Ingredients

1⅓ cups almond flour
10 oz Spanish manchego cheese, grated
Salt and black pepper to taste
1 tsp garlic powder
4 tbsp olive oil
⅓ tsp sweet paprika
⅓ cup heavy cream

Directions

Mix the almond flour, manchego cheese, salt, pepper, garlic powder, and paprika in a bowl. Add in the olive oil and mix well. Top with the heavy cream and mix again until a smooth, thick mixture has formed. Add 1 to 2 tablespoon of water, if it is too thick.

Place the dough on a cutting board and cover with plastic wrap. Use a rolling pin to spread out the dough into a light rectangle. Cut cracker squares out of the dough and arrange them on a baking sheet without overlapping. Bake in the oven for 20 minutes at 350°F; serve chilled.

Crispy Zucchini Sticks

Total Time: 20 minutes | Serves: 4

Per serving: Calories 180, Fat 14g; Net Carbs 2g; Protein 6g

Ingredients

- 1 tsp smoked paprika
- ¼ cup pork rind crumbs
- ¼ cup Pecorino Romano cheese, shredded
- Salt and chili pepper to taste
- 3 fresh eggs
- 4 zucchinis, cut into strips

Aioli:
- ½ cup mayonnaise
- 1 garlic clove, minced
- Juice and zest from ½ lemon

Directions

Line a baking sheet with foil. Grease with cooking spray and set aside.

Mix the pork rinds, smoked paprika, Pecorino Romano cheese, salt, and chili pepper in a bowl. Beat the eggs in another bowl. Coat zucchini strips in egg, then in cheese mixture, and arrange on the baking sheet. Grease lightly with cooking spray and bake in the oven for 15 minutes at 425°F to be crispy.

Combine in a bowl mayonnaise, lemon juice, and garlic, and gently stir until everything is well incorporated. Add the lemon zest, adjust the seasoning and stir again. Cover and place in the refrigerator until ready to serve. Serve the zucchini strips with garlic aioli for dipping.

Parsley & Garlic Celeriac Mash

Total Time: 30 minutes | Serves: 4

Per serving: Calories 94, Fat 0.5g; Net Carbs 6g; Protein 2.4g

Ingredients

4 cups celeriac, chopped
4 cups water
2 oz mascarpone, at room temperature
2 tbsp olive oil
⅓ cup Greek yogurt
½ tsp garlic powder
2 tsp fresh parsley
Salt and black pepper to taste

Directions

Boil the celeriac in salted water for 5 minutes over high heat, then reduce the heat to low to simmer for 15 minutes. Drain the celeriac through a colander after.

Pour the celeriac in a bowl, add the mascarpone, olive oil, Greek yogurt, garlic powder, salt, and pepper. Mash with potato masher until well combined. Serve sprinkled with parsley.

Green Bean Crisps

Total Time: 30 minutes | Serves: 2

Per serving: Calories 210, Fat 19g; Net Carbs 3g; Protein 5g

Ingredients

¼ cup Grana Padano cheese, shredded
2 cups green beans, thread removed
¼ cup pork rind crumbs
1 tsp garlic powder
Salt and black pepper to taste
2 eggs

Directions

Line two baking sheets with foil. Grease with cooking spray and set aside.

Mix the cheese, pork rinds, garlic powder, salt, and black pepper in a bowl. Beat the eggs in another bowl. Coat green beans in eggs, then cheese mixture and arrange evenly on the baking sheets.

Grease lightly with cooking spray and bake in the oven for 15 minutes at 425°F to be crispy. Transfer to a wire rack to cool before serving.

Greek Zucchini Chips

Total Time: 52 minutes | Serves: 4

Per serving: Calories 253, Fat 19.4g; Net Carbs 3.8g; Protein 14.5g

Ingredients

1 cup plain Greek yogurt
12 oz feta cheese, crumbled
¼ cup dill, chopped
1 tbsp garlic, minced
4 zucchinis, thinly sliced

⅓ cup almond flour
½ cup grated Parmesan cheese
Salt and black pepper to taste
2 tbsp olive oil

Directions

Preheat the oven to 450°F. Grease a baking sheet with olive oil and set aside.

In the food processor, add the Greek yogurt, feta cheese, dill, and garlic. Blend the ingredients for 2 minutes. Pour into a bowl and season with salt and pepper. Place the bowl in the refrigerator to chill while you make the chips.

Mix the almond flour, Parmesan cheese, salt, and pepper in a bowl. Then dip and press each zucchini slice in the flour mixture on both sides; coating generously. Place on the baking sheet and cook in the oven for 25 to 30 minutes. Remove when ready and plate.

Mascarpone & Bresaola Roll

Total Time: 40 minutes | Serves: 4

Per serving: Calories 266, Fat 24g; Net Carbs 0g; Protein 13g

Ingredients

8 oz mascarpone cheese
10 oz bresaola, sliced

10 canned pepperoncini peppers, sliced

Directions

On a flat surface, Lay a plastic wrap and arrange the bresaola slices all over slightly overlapping each other. Spread the cheese on top of the bresaola layers and arrange the pepperoncini on top. Hold two opposite ends of the plastic wrap and roll the pastrami. Twist both ends to tighten and refrigerate for 2 hours. Unwrap the bresaola roll and slice into 2-inch pieces; serve.

Ricotta Filled Piquillos

Total Time: 20 minutes | Serves: 8

Per serving: Calories 132, Fat: 11g; Net Carbs: 2.5g; Protein: 6g

Ingredients

1 tbsp olive oil
8 canned roasted piquillo peppers
Filling:
8 oz ricotta cheese
3 tbsp heavy cream
3 tbsp parsley, chopped

3 slices jamon serrano
1 tbsp balsamic vinegar

1 garlic clove, minced
1 tbsp olive oil
1 tbsp mint, chopped

Directions

Combine all filling ingredients in a bowl. Place in a freezer bag, press down and squeeze, and cut off the bottom. Drain and deseed the peppers. Squeeze about 2 tbsp of the filling into each pepper. Wrap a jamon serrano slice onto each pepper. Secure with toothpicks. Arrange them on a serving platter. Sprinkle the olive oil and vinegar over.

Mozzarella Biscuits

Total Time: 20 minutes | Serves: 4

Per serving: Calories 306, Fat 27.6g; Net Carbs 0.9g; Protein 10.9g

Ingredients

⅓ cup almond flour
2 tsp garlic powder
Salt to taste
1 tsp baking powder

5 eggs
⅓ cup butter, melted
1¼ cups mozzarella cheese, grated
⅓ cup sour cream

Directions

Mix the almond flour, garlic powder, salt, baking powder, and mozzarella cheese, in a bowl.

In a separate bowl, whisk the eggs, butter, and sour cream, and then pour the resulting mixture into the dry ingredients. Stir well until a dough-like consistency has formed.

Fetch half soupspoon of the mixture onto a baking sheet with 2-inch intervals between each batter. Bake for 12 minutes at 350ºF to be golden brown. Let cool before serving.

Effortless Spinach Balls

Total Time: 30 minutes | Serves: 8

Per serving: Calories 160, Fat: 15g; Net Carbs: 0.8g; Protein: 8g

Ingredients

⅓ cup feta cheese, crumbled
¼ tsp nutmeg
¼ tsp pepper
3 tbsp heavy cream
1 tbsp onion powder

2 tbsp butter, melted
⅓ cup Parmesan cheese
2 eggs
8 oz spinach
1 cup almond flour

Directions

Preheat the oven to 350°F.

Place all ingredients in a food processor. Process until smooth. Place in the freezer for about 10 minutes. Make balls out of the mixture and arrange them on a lined baking sheet. Bake for 10-12 minutes.

Stuffed Avocado with Tuna

Total Time: 20 minutes | Serves: 4

Per serving: Calories: 286; Fat 23.9g; Net Carbs 9g; Protein 11.2g

Ingredients

2 avocados, halved and pitted
4 oz mozzarella cheese, grated
2 tbsp capers
2 oz canned tuna, flaked

2 tbsp chives, chopped
Salt and black pepper, to taste
½ cup curly endive, chopped

Directions

Set avocado halves in an ovenproof dish. Mix chives, black pepper, salt, capers, and tuna. Stuff the tuna mixture in avocado halves. Top with grated cheese. Bake in the oven for 15 minutes at 360°F or until the top is golden brown.

Feta Balls with Spring Salad

Total Time: 20 minutes | Serves: 6

Per serving: Calories: 234; Fat 16.7g; Net Carbs 7.9g; Protein 12.4g

Ingredients

For the Cheese Balls:

3 eggs
1½ cups feta cheese, crumbled
1 cup almond flour
1 tbsp flax meal
1 tsp baking powder
Salt and black pepper, to taste

For the Salad:

1 head romaine lettuce
½ cup cucumber, thinly sliced
2 tomatoes, seeded and chopped
½ red onion, thinly sliced
10 radishes, thinly sliced
⅓ cup mayonnaise
1 tsp mustard
Salt, to taste

Directions

Line a piece of parchment paper to a baking sheet. In a mixing dish, mix all ingredients for the cheese balls; form balls out of the mixture. Set the balls on the prepared baking sheet. Bake for 10 minutes at 390°F until crisp. Arrange lettuce leaves on a large salad platter; add in radishes, tomatoes, cucumbers, and red onion.

Using a small mixing bowl, mix the mayonnaise, salt, and mustard. Sprinkle this mixture over the vegetables. Add cheese balls on top and serve.

Arugula & Ricotta Gnocchi

Total Time: 13 minutes | Serves: 4

Per serving: Calories 125, Fat 8.3g; Net Carbs 4.1g; Protein 6.5g

Ingredients

3 cups arugula, chopped
1 cup ricotta cheese
1 cup Parmesan cheese, grated
¼ tsp nutmeg powder
1 egg
Salt and black pepper
4 tbsp almond flour
2 ½ cups water
2 tbsp olive oil

Directions

Crack the egg in a bowl, add the ricotta cheese, half of the parmesan cheese, nutmeg powder, salt, arugula, almond flour, and pepper. Mix well. Make quenelles of the mixture using 2 tbsp and set aside.

Bring the water to boil over high heat, about 5 minutes. Place one gnocchi onto the water, if it breaks apart; add some more flour to the other gnocchi to firm it up.

Put the remaining gnocchi in the water to poach and rise to the top, about 2 minutes. Remove to a serving plate. Melt the butter in a microwave and pour over the gnocchi. Sprinkle with the remaining parmesan cheese and serve with green salad.

Mushroom Cheesy Balls

Total Time: 20 minutes | Serves: 4

Per serving: Calories 370; Fat: 30g; Net Carbs: 7.7g; Protein: 16.8g

Ingredients

2 tbsp olive oil
2 garlic cloves, minced
2 cups cremini mushrooms, chopped
4 tbsp almond flour
4 tbsp ground flax seeds
4 tbsp hemp seeds
4 tbsp sunflower seeds
1 tbsp Italian seasonings
1 tsp mustard
2 eggs, whisked
½ cup pecorino cheese, grated

Directions

Warm olive oil in a pan over medium heat. Add in mushrooms and garlic and sauté until there is no more water in mushrooms.

Place in pecorino cheese, almond flour, hemp seeds, mustard, eggs, sunflower seeds, flax seeds, and Italian seasonings. Create 4 burgers from the mixture.

In a pan, warm the remaining butter; fry the burgers for 7 minutes. Flip them over with a wide spatula and cook for 6 more minutes.

Herby Stuffed Eggs

Total Time: 30 minutes | Serves: 3

Per serving: Calories 258, Fat 19.3g; Net Carbs 2.7g; Protein 12.9g

Ingredients

6 large eggs
6 tbsp mayonnaise
Salt and chili pepper to taste
1 tsp herbes de Provence
¼ tsp Dijon mustard
¼ tsp sweet paprika
Chopped parsley to garnish

Directions

Cover the eggs with salted water, and bring to boil on high heat for 10 minutes. Cut the eggs in half lengthways and remove the yolks into a medium bowl. Use a fork to crush the yolks.

Add the mayonnaise, salt, chili pepper, herbes de Provence, mustard, and paprika. Mix together until a smooth paste has formed. Then, spoon the mixture into the piping bag and fill the egg white holes with it. Garnish with the chopped parsley and serve immediately.

Meaty Vegetable Tart

Total Time: 45 minutes | Serves: 6

Per serving: Calories 310; Fat: 18.3g; Net Carbs: 3.8g; Protein: 30.7g

Ingredients

1 pound ground beef
1 onion, chopped
1 garlic clove, minced
6 asparagus, chopped
Salt and black pepper to taste
4 zucchinis, sliced
4 tomatoes, sliced
¼ cup whipping cream
8 eggs
½ cup mozzarella cheese, grated

Directions

Grease a baking dish with cooking spray. In a bowl, mix onion, asparagus, ground beef, garlic, pepper and salt. Layer the meat mixture on the bottom of the baking dish. Spread zucchini slices on top followed with tomato slices.

In a separate bowl, combine cheese, eggs and whipping cream. Top with this creamy mixture and bake in the oven for 40 minutes at 360°F, until the edges and top become brown.

Catalan Salsa Aioli

Total Time: 10 minutes | Serves: 6

Per serving: Calories 116; Fat: 13.2g; Net Carbs: 0.2g; Protein: 0.4g

Ingredients

Juice of 1 lemon
3 egg yolks, at room temperature
1 clove garlic, crushed
Salt and black pepper to taste
½ cup extra virgin olive oil
¼ cup fresh parsley, chopped

Directions

In a deep bowl, place in salt, black pepper, lemon juice, garlic, and egg yolks; pulse well to get a smooth and creamy mixture. Set blender to slow speed. Slowly sprinkle in olive oil and combine to ensure the oil incorporates well. Stir in parsley. Refrigerate until ready to use.

Scallions and Cheese Stuffed Tomatoes

Total Time: 35 minutes | Serves: 4

Per serving: Calories 306; Fat: 27.5g; Net Carbs: 4.4g; Protein: 11.3g

Ingredients

4 tomatoes
4 slices feta cheese
¼ cup full-fat yogurt
1 egg, whisked
1 clove garlic, minced
4 tbsp fresh scallions, chopped
Salt and black pepper, to taste
2 tbsp olive oil

Directions

Lightly grease a rimmed baking sheet with cooking spray. Horizontally slice tomatoes into halves; scoop out pulp and seeds.

In a bowl, mix egg, salt, olive oil, black pepper, garlic, yogurt, and scallions. Split the filling between tomatoes, cover each one with a feta slice and bake in the oven for 30 minutes at 360°F. Place on a wire rack and allow to cool for 5 minutes; serve alongside fresh rocket leaves.

Mascarpone & Carrot Mousse

Total Time: 15 min + cooling time | Serves: 6

Per serving: Calories 368, Fat: 33.7g; Net Carbs: 5.6g; Protein: 13.8g

Ingredients

1½ cups half & half
½ cup mascarpone
½ cup xylitol
3 eggs
1¼ cups canned carrots
½ tsp ground cloves
½ tsp ground cinnamon
¼ tsp grated nutmeg
A pinch of salt

Directions

In a saucepan over medium heat, mix xylitol, mascarpone, and half & half, and boil. Beat the eggs; slowly place in ½ of the hot cream mixture to the beaten eggs.

Pour the mixture back to the pan. Cook for 2 to 4 minutes, until thick. Kill the heat; add in carrots, cinnamon, salt, nutmeg, and cloves. Blend with a blender and split the mixture among serving plates and refrigerate.

DINNER RECIPES

Mediterranean Chicken Breasts

Total Time: 65 minutes | Serves: 6

Per serving: Calories 430, Fat 23g; Net Carbs 3g; Protein 33g

Ingredients

2 tsp butter
3 tsp olive oil
3 medium lemons, sliced
1½ lb chicken breasts, halved
Salt and black pepper to season

4 tbsp almond flour
2 tbsp capers, rinsed
1¼ cup chicken broth
1½ tbsp chopped fresh parsley
Parsley for garnish

Directions

Lay a piece of parchment paper on a baking sheet. Preheat the oven to 350°F.

Lay the lemon slices on the baking sheet, drizzle them with olive oil and sprinkle with salt. Roast in the oven for 25 minutes to brown the lemon rinds.

Cover the chicken with plastic wrap, place them on a flat surface, and gently pound with the rolling pin to flatten to about ½-inch thickness.

Remove the plastic wraps and season the chicken with salt and pepper.

Dredge the chicken in the almond flour on each side, and shake off any excess flour. Set aside.

Heat the olive oil in a skillet over medium heat and fry the chicken on both sides to a golden brown, for about 8 minutes in total.

Then, pour the chicken broth in, shake the skillet, and let the broth boil and reduce to a thick consistency, about 12 minutes.

Lightly stir in the capers, roasted lemon, pepper, butter, and parsley, and simmer on low heat for 10 minutes. Serve the chicken with the sauce and sprinkled parsley.

French Chicken Packets

Total Time: 48 minutes | Serves: 4

Per serving: Calories 436, Fat 27.3g; Net Carbs 0.8g; Protein 34.1g

Ingredients

1 pound chicken breasts, skinless, scored
4 tbsp butter
2 tbsp olive oil + extra for drizzling
4 tbsp white wine
2 tbsp Dijon mustard
3 cups portobello mushrooms, teared up
½ cup celery, chopped
2 cups water
3 cloves garlic, minced
4 sprigs thyme, chopped
3 lemons, juiced
Salt and black pepper to taste

Directions

Preheat the oven to 450°F. Spread the celery on a baking sheet, drizzle with oil, and bake for 20 minutes. In a bowl, evenly mix the chicken, roasted celery, mushrooms, garlic, thyme, lemon juice, salt, pepper, and mustard. Make 4 large cuts of foil, fold them in half, and then fold them in half again. Tightly fold the two open edges together to create a bag.

Share the chicken mixture into each bag, drizzle with the white wine, olive oil, and top with a tablespoon each of butter on each. Seal the last open end securely making sure not to pierce the bag. Put the bag on a baking tray and bake the chicken in the middle of the oven for 25 minutes.

Spanish Chorizo Chicken Paella

Total Time: 63 minutes | Serves: 6

Per serving: Calories 771, Fat 54.2g; Net Carbs 2.7g; Protein 58.4g

Ingredients

12 chicken drumsticks
8 oz Spanish chorizo, sliced
1 onion, chopped
½ red bell pepper, cut into chunks
2 tbsp olive oil
½ cup parsley, chopped
½ tsp turmeric
1 tsp smoked paprika
2 tbsp tomato puree
½ cup white wine
1 cup chicken broth
2 cups cauli rice
1 cup chopped green beans
1 lemon, cut in wedges
Salt and pepper, to taste

Directions

Heat the olive oil in a cast iron pan over medium heat, season the chicken with salt and pepper, and fry on both sides for 10 minutes to lightly brown. Remove to a plate.

Add the chorizo and onion and sauté for 4 minutes. Include the tomato puree, bell pepper, and paprika, and let simmer for 2 minutes. Add the broth and turmeric, and bring the ingredients to boil for 6 minutes until slightly reduced. Stir in the cauli rice, white wine, green beans, half of the parsley, and lay the chicken on top. Cook for 20 minutes. Let the paella sit to cool for 10 minutes before serving garnished with the remaining parsley and lemon wedges.

Tomato and Eggplant Braised Chicken Thighs

Total Time: 45 minutes | Serves: 4

Per serving: Calories 468, Fat 39.5g; Net Carbs 2g; Protein 26g

Ingredients

12 chicken thighs
2 tbsp olive oil
Salt and black pepper to taste
2 cloves garlic, minced
2 cups plum tomatoes, chopped
1 eggplant, peeled and chopped
10 fresh basil leaves, chopped + extra to garnish

Directions

Warm olive oil in a saucepan over medium heat, season the chicken with salt and black pepper, and fry for 4 minutes on each side until golden brown. Remove chicken to a plate. Sauté the garlic in the same oil for 2 minutes, pour in the tomatoes, and cook covered for 8 minutes.

Add in the eggplant and basil. Cook for 4 minutes. Season the sauce with salt and black pepper, stir and add the chicken. Coat with sauce and simmer for 3 minutes. Garnish with basil and serve.

Lemon-Marinated Chicken Kebabs

Total Time: 2 hours 17 minutes | Serves: 4

Per serving: Calories 350, Fat 11g; Net Carbs 3.5g; Protein 34g

Ingredients

1 pound chicken breasts, cut into cubes
2 tbsp olive oil
2 cloves garlic, minced
½ cup lemon juice
Salt and black pepper to taste
1 tsp fresh rosemary, chopped to garnish
1 lemon, cut into wedges to garnish

Directions

Thread the chicken onto skewers and set aside. In a bowl, mix half of the oil, garlic, salt, pepper, and lemon juice, and add the chicken skewers. Cover the bowl and let the chicken marinate for at least 2 hours in the refrigerator.

When the marinating time is almost over, preheat a grill to 350°F, and remove the chicken onto the grill. Cook for 6 minutes on each side. Remove and serve warm garnished with rosemary leaves and lemons wedges.

Veggie Chicken Drumsticks with Tomato Sauce

Total Time: 1 hour 35 minutes | Serves: 4

Per serving: Calories 515, Fat 34.2g; Net Carbs 7.3g; Protein 50.8g

Ingredients

1 white onion, chopped
2 turnips, peeled and diced
4 baby carrots, chopped in 1-inch pieces
2 bell peppers, seeded, cut into chunks
2 cloves garlic, minced
8 chicken drumsticks
1½ tbsp olive oil
¼ cup almond flour
1 cup chicken broth
1 (28 oz) can tomato sauce, sugar-free
2 tbsp dried Italian herbs
Salt and black pepper to taste

Directions

Heat the oil in a skillet over medium heat, season the drumsticks with salt and pepper, and fry on both sides for 10 minutes. Remove to a baking dish. Sauté the onion, turnips, bell peppers, carrots, and garlic in the same oil and cook for 10 minutes, stirring often.

Preheat oven to 400°F.

In a bowl, evenly combine the broth, coconut flour, tomato paste, and Italian herbs together, and pour it over the vegetables in the pan. Stir and cook to thicken for 4 minutes. Pour the mixture on the chicken in the baking dish. Bake the chicken and vegetables in the oven for around 1 hour.

Turkey Meatballs with Squash Pasta

Total Time: 65 minutes | Serves: 6

Per serving: Calories 728, Fat 43.3g; Net Carbs 7.8g; Protein 68.9g

Ingredients

2 lb butternut squash, halved
2 lb ground turkey
Salt and black pepper to taste
1 cup pork rinds, crushed
4 cloves garlic, minced
1 onion, chopped
2 stalks celery, chopped

2 tbsp parsley leaves, chopped
3 tbsp olive oil + extra for brushing
1 egg
2 cups sugar-free tomato sauce
10 leaves basil, chopped
1 cup Parmesan cheese, grated
2 tbsp Parmesan cheese, grated to serve

Directions

Scoop the seeds out of the squash halves with a spoon. Sprinkle with salt and brush with olive oil. Place in a baking dish and cover with foil. Roast for 20 minutes at 450°F, then remove the aluminum foil and continue cooking for 35 minutes. When ready, scrape the pulp into strands. Remove the spaghetti strands to a bowl and toss with 2 tbsp of Parmesan cheese. Season with salt, and plate.

Add the garlic, onion, celery, and parsley into the food processor, and blend into a smooth paste for about 2 minutes. Put the ground turkey in a bowl; pour in half of the celery puree, pork rinds, egg, and a cup of Parmesan cheese; mix well. Mold out meatballs from the mixture and place them on a baking sheet. Bake the meatballs for just 10 minutes, but not done.

Place a pot over medium heat and warm 3 tbsp of olive oil. Stir-fry the remaining vegetable paste for 5 minutes. Stir in the tomato sauce, basil, and salt to taste. Let the sauce cook on low-medium heat for 5 minutes, remove, and add in the meatballs. Continue cooking for 15 minutes. Spoon the meatballs with sauce over the spaghetti, sprinkle with extra Parmesan cheese and serve.

Bresaola & Gorgonzola Cakes

Total Time: 25 minutes | Serves: 5

Per serving: Calories 240, Fat: 15.3g; Net Carbs: 10g; Protein: 16.1g

Ingredients

- 2 tbsp olive oil
- ½ cup almond flour
- 3 slices bresaola, chopped
- 4 eggs, beaten
- 1 tsp baking powder
- 1 cup gorgonzola cheese
- ¼ tsp salt
- ¼ tsp grated nutmeg

Directions

Preheat the oven to 390°F. In a deep bowl mix all the ingredients, except for the olive oil until well combined. Grease cake molds with the olive oil, fill them with batter (¾ full) and bake for 15 minutes. Let cool completely before serving.

Chicken Breasts Stuffed with Parma Ham

Total Time: 40 minutes | Serves: 4

Per serving: Calories 536, Fat 37.7g; Net Carbs 1.3g; Protein 4.24g

Ingredients

- 1 pound chicken breasts
- 2 tbsp olive oil
- 2 cloves garlic, minced
- 1 red onion, chopped
- 4 tbsp dried mixed herbs
- 4 oz Parma ham, sliced
- 8 oz mascarpone, at room temperature
- 2 lemons, zested
- Salt and black pepper to taste

Directions

Heat the oil in a small skillet and sauté the garlic and red onion with a pinch of salt and lemon zest for 3 minutes. Turn the heat off and let it cool. After, stir the mascarpone and mixed herbs into the onion mixture.

Score a pocket in each chicken breast, fill the holes with the cream cheese mixture and cover with the cut-out chicken. Wrap each breast with two Parma ham slices and secure the ends with a toothpick.

Preheat the oven to 350°F.

Lay the chicken parcels on a greased baking sheet and cook in the oven for 20 minutes. After cooking, remove to rest for 4 minutes before serving with a green salad and roasted tomatoes.

One-Pot Chicken and Broccoli

Total Time: 20 minutes | Serves: 4

Per serving: Calories 286, Fat 10.1g; Net Carbs 3.4g; Protein 17.3g

Ingredients

1 pound chicken breasts, cut into strips
3 tbsp olive oil
2 tsp balsamic vinegar
1 tsp xylitol
2 tsp xanthan gum

1 lemon, juiced
1 cup unsalted walnuts
2 cups broccoli florets
1 white onion, thinly sliced
Pepper to taste

Directions

In a bowl, mix the vinegar, lemon juice, xylitol, and xanthan gum. Set aside.

Heat the oil in a wok and fry the walnuts for 2 minutes until golden-brown.

Remove the walnuts to a paper towel-lined plate and set aside. Sauté the onion in the same oil for 4 minutes until soft and browned; add to the walnuts.

Add the chicken to the wok and cook for 4 minutes; include the broccoli and pepper. Stir-fry and pour the soy sauce mixture in.

Stir and cook the sauce for 4 minutes and pour in the walnuts and onion. Stir once more, cook for 1 minute, and turn the heat off. Serve the chicken stir-fry with green salad.

Gorgonzola Stuffed Bell Peppers

Total Time: 45 minutes | Serves: 4

Per serving: Calories 359; Fat: 29.7g; Net Carbs: 6.7g; Protein: 17.7g

Ingredients

2 tbsp olive oil
6 oz gorgonzola cheese, crumbled
4 red bell peppers, blanched
6 oz cottage cheese
½ cup pork rinds, crushed
2 cloves garlic, smashed

1½ cups tomatoes, pureed
1 tsp dried basil
Salt and black pepper, to taste
½ tsp chili pepper
½ oregano

Directions

Preheat oven to 360°F.

Lightly grease the sides and bottom of a casserole dish with olive oil.

In a bowl, mix garlic, cottage cheese, pork rinds, and gorgonzola cheese. Stuff the peppers and add to the casserole dish.

Combine the tomato puree with oregano, salt, cayenne pepper, black pepper, and basil. Scatter the tomato mixture over stuffed peppers; use a foil to cover the dish. Bake for 40 minutes until the peppers are tender.

Chicken Wings with Parmesan & Yogurt Sauce

Total Time: 25 minutes | Serves: 6

Per serving: Calories 452, Fat 36.4g; Net Carbs 4g; Protein 24g

Ingredients

Wings

2 pounds chicken wings
½ cup olive oil
Salt and black pepper to taste

Yogurt Sauce

1 cup plain yogurt
1 tsp fresh lemon juice

Cooking spray
½ cup Hot sauce
¼ cup Parmesan cheese, grated

Salt and black pepper to taste

Directions

Preheat oven to 400°F and season wings with salt and pepper. Line them on a baking sheet and grease with cooking spray. Bake for 20 minutes until golden brown.

Mix the yogurt, lemon juice, salt, and black pepper in a bowl. Chill while making the chicken.

Mix olive oil, hot sauce, and parmesan in a bowl. Toss chicken in the sauce to evenly coat and plate. Serve with yogurt dipping sauce.

Grilled Asparagus with Pancetta Wrapped Chicken

Total Time: 48 minutes | Serves: 4

Per serving: Calories 570, Fat 38g; Net Carbs 2g; Protein 49.9g

Ingredients

1 pound chicken breasts, boneless
8 pancetta slices
1 lb asparagus spears
4 tbsp olive oil

Salt and black pepper to taste
2 tbsp fresh lemon juice
Pecorino cheese for topping

Directions

Season chicken breasts with salt and black pepper, and wrap 2 pancetta slices around each chicken breast.

Preheat oven to 370°F.

Arrange on a baking sheet that is lined with parchment paper, drizzle with 2 tbsp of olive oil and bake for 25-30 minutes until bacon is brown and crispy.

Preheat your grill on high heat. Brush the asparagus spears with the remaining olive oil and season with salt. Grill for 8-10 minutes, frequently turning until slightly charred. Remove to a plate and drizzle with lemon juice. Grate over Pecorino so that it melts a little on contact with the hot asparagus and forms a cheesy dressing.

Spring Omelet

Total Time: 15 minutes | Serves: 2

Per serving: Calories 319; Fat: 25g; Net Carbs: 10g; Protein: 14.9g

Ingredients

2 tsp olive oil
2 spring onions, chopped
2 spring garlic, chopped
4 eggs, beaten
1 cup yogurt
2 tomatoes, sliced
1 green chili pepper, minced
2 tbsp fresh basil, chopped
Salt and black pepper, to taste

Directions

Set a pan over high heat and warm the olive oil. Sauté garlic and onions until tender.

Whisk the eggs with yogurt. Pour into the pan and cook until eggs become puffy and brown to bottom. Add basil, chili pepper and tomatoes to one side of the omelet. Add in pepper and salt. Fold the omelet in half and slice into wedges.

Omelet Flambé

Total Time: 10 minutes | Serves: 3

Per serving: Calories 488, Fat: 42g; Net Carbs: 8g; Protein: 15.3g

Ingredients

6 eggs, beaten
¼ cup heavy cream
½ tsp ground cloves
1 tbsp olive oil
2 tbsp mascarpone cheese
18 fresh blueberries
1 tbsp powdered swerve
1 tbsp brandy

Directions

Set pan over medium heat and warm oil. Mix the eggs with ground cloves and heavy cream. Place in the egg mixture; cook for 3 minutes. Set the omelet onto a plate; apply a topping of blueberries and mascarpone cheese. Roll it up and sprinkle with powdered swerve. Pour the warm brandy over the omelet and ignite it. Let the flame die out and serve.

Five Spices Chicken Kabobs

Total Time: 80 minutes | Serves: 6

Per serving: Calories 198, Fat: 13.5g; Net Carbs: 3.1g; Protein: 17.5g

Ingredients

6 chicken breasts, cubed
2 red bell peppers chopped
2 tbsp olive oil
2 tbsp five spice powder
2 tbsp яwerve sweetener
1 tbsp Worcestershire sauce

Directions

Combine the sauce and seasonings in a bowl. Add the chicken, and let marinate for 1 hour in the fridge. Preheat the grill. Take 12 skewers and thread the chicken and bell peppers. Grill for 3 minutes per side.

Cheese Turkey with White Sauce

Total Time: 20 minutes | Serves: 4

Per serving: Calories 416; Fat: 26g; Net Carbs: 3.2g; Protein: 40.7g

Ingredients

8 oz mozzarella cheese, shredded
1 tbsp olive oil
1 pound turkey breasts, sliced
2 garlic cloves, minced
½ cup heavy cream
⅓ cup chicken broth
2 tbsp tomato paste
1 tbsp fresh parsley, chopped

Directions

Set a pan over medium heat and warm the oil; add in garlic and turkey and fry for 4 minutes; set aside. Stir in the broth, tomato paste, and heavy cream; cook until thickened.

Return the turkey to the pan; spread shredded cheese over. Let sit for 5 minutes while covered or until the cheese melts. Serve sprinkled with parsley.

Stuffed Chicken Breasts with Basil Tomato Sauce

Total Time: 45 minutes | Serves: 6

Per serving: Calories 412, Fat: 19.7g; Net Carbs: 2g; Protein: 49.6g

Ingredients

½ cup cottage cheese
¼ cup yogurt
6 mozzarella slices
2 cups kale, chopped
⅓ cup mozzarella, shredded
1 tbsp olive oil
1 cup tomato basil sauce
1½ pounds chicken breasts

Directions

Combine the cottage cheese, yogurt, shredded mozzarella, and kale in the microwave. Cut the chicken with the knife a couple of times horizontally. Stuff with the filling. Brush the top with olive oil.

Place on a lined baking dish and in the oven. Bake the chicken in the oven for 25 minutes at 400°F. Pour the tomato basil sauce over and top with mozzarella slices. Return to oven and cook for 5 minutes until the cheese melts.

One-Pot Rosemary Chicken Thighs

Total Time: 1 hour 20 minutes | Serves: 4

Per serving: Calories 477, Fat: 31g; Net Carbs: 2.5g; Protein: 31g

Ingredients

1 pound chicken thighs
Salt and black pepper to taste
1 lemon, juiced and zested
2 tbsp olive oil
1 tbsp fresh rosemary, chopped
1 garlic clove, minced

Directions

Combine all ingredients except for the rosemary in a bowl. Place in the fridge for one hour. Heat a skillet over medium heat. Add the chicken along with the juices and cook until crispy, about 7 minutes per side. Serve sprinkled with fresh rosemary.

Herbs Stuffed Roast Chicken

Total Time: 70 minutes | Serves: 8

Per serving: Calories 432, Fat: 32g; Net Carbs: 5.1g; Protein: 30g

Ingredients

4 pounds whole chicken
1 handful of oregano
1 handful of thyme
1 handful of parsley
1 tbsp olive oil
2 pounds cabbage, shredded
1 lemon
4 tbsp butter

Directions

Stuff the chicken with oregano, thyme, and lemon. Make sure the wings are tucked over and behind. Preheat the oven to 450°F. Roast the chicken for 15 minutes. Reduce the heat to 325°F and cook for 20 minutes.

Spread the butter over the chicken, and sprinkle parsley; add the cabbage. Return to the oven and bake for 30 more minutes. Let sit for 10 minutes before carving.

Chili & Sage Flattened Chicken

Total Time: 15 minutes | Serves: 6

Per serving: Calories 265, Fat 9g; Net Carbs 3g; Protein 26g

Ingredients

1½ pounds chicken breasts
2 cloves garlic, minced
½ cup sage leaves, chopped
3 lemons, juiced
4 tbsp olive oil
¼ cup xylitol
Salt and black pepper to taste
3 small chilies, minced

Directions

In a bowl, mix the garlic, sage, lemon Juice, olive oil, salt, black pepper, and xylitol. Set aside.

Cover the chicken with plastic wraps, and use the rolling pin to pound to ½-inch thickness. Remove the wrap afterward, and brush the mixture on the chicken on both sides.

Preheat a grill to 350°F. Place on the grill, cover the lid and cook for 5 minutes. Baste the chicken with more of the spice mixture, and continue cooking for 5 more minutes.

Turkey Soup with Zoodles

Total Time: 45 minutes | Serves: **5**

Per serving: Calories 305, Fat 11g; Net Carbs 3g; Protein 15g

Ingredients

3 celery stalks, chopped
2 shallots, chopped
1 tbsp olive oil
6 cups chicken stock
Salt and black pepper to taste
2 tbsp fresh parsley, chopped
2 zucchinis, spiralized
1 pound turkey breasts, cooked and chopped

Directions

Set a pot over medium heat, stir in shallots and celery and cook for 5 minutes. Place in the parsley, turkey meat, black pepper, salt, and stock, and cook for 20 minutes. Stir in the zoodles, and cook turkey soup for 5 minutes. Serve in bowls and enjoy.

Cheesy Spinach Chicken Bake

Total Time: 45 minutes | Serves: 6

Per serving: Calories 340, Fat 30.2g; Net Carbs 3.1g; Protein 15g

Ingredients

2 lb chicken breasts, boneless and skinless
1¼ cups mozzarella cheese, shredded
1 tsp Italian seasoning
Sea salt and black pepper to taste
2 cups fresh baby spinach
3 tsp olive oil
½ cup cream cheese, at room temperature
4 tbsp water

Directions

Season chicken with Italian seasoning, salt, and black pepper. Put in the baking dish and layer spinach over the chicken. Mix olive oil with cream cheese, mozzarella, salt, and black pepper and stir in water. Pour the mixture over the chicken; cover with aluminium foil.

Bake for 20 minutes at 370°F, remove foil and continue cooking for 15 minutes until a nice golden brown color is formed on top. Take out and allow sitting for 5 minutes.

Delicious Chicken Goujons

Total Time: 25 minutes | Serves: 2

Per serving: Calories 875, Fat 74.4g; Net Carbs 2.3g; Protein 43g

Ingredients

½ pound chicken breasts, cubed
½ cup almond flour
1 egg, beaten

2 tbsp garlic powder
Salt and black pepper, to taste
½ cup olive oil

Directions

In a bowl, whisk together salt, garlic powder, almond flour, and black pepper, until combined. To the beaten egg, add the chicken cubes, then in the flour mixture. Set a pan over medium heat and warm olive oil, add in the chicken nuggets, and cook for 6 minutes on each side. Remove to paper towels, drain the excess grease and serve.

Marvellous Turkey Meatballs

Total Time: 15 minutes | Serves: 4

Per serving: Calories 310, Fat: 26g; Net Carbs: 2g; Protein: 22g

Ingredients

1 lb ground turkey
6 sun-dried tomatoes, chopped
10 fresh basil leaves, chopped
½ cup provolone cheese, shredded
½ tsp Italian seasoning

1 tbsp Dijon mustard
1 egg
Salt and black pepper to taste
¼ cup almond flour
2 tbsp olive oil

Directions

Place everything except the oil in a bowl. Mix with your hands until combined. Form 16 meatballs out of the mixture. Heat olive oil in a skillet over medium heat. Cook the meatballs for 3 minutes per each side. Serve with zucchini spaghetti and tomato sauce.

Mustard Chicken Thighs

Total Time: 30 minutes | Serves: 4

Per serving: Calories 528, Fat: 42g; Net Carbs: 4g; Protein: 33g

Ingredients

1 onion, chopped
½ cup chicken stock
1 tbsp olive oil
1 pound chicken thighs
¼ cup heavy cream
2 tbsp Dijon mustard
1 tsp thyme
1 garlic clove, pressed

Directions

Heat the olive oil in a pan. Cook the chicken for about 4 minutes per side. Set aside. Sauté the onion in the same pan for 3 minutes, add the stock, and simmer for 5 minutes. Stir in mustard and heavy cream, along with thyme and garlic powder. Pour the sauce over the chicken and serve.

Baked Breaded Chicken

Total Time: 50 minutes | Serves: 6

Per serving: Calories: 465, Fat: 31g; Net Carbs: 2.6g; Protein: 33g

Ingredients

1½ pounds chicken breasts, sliced
Salt and black pepper, to taste
4 oz mayonnaise
2 oz Dijon mustard
1 tsp erythritol
1 cup pork rinds, crushed
¾ cup Grana-Padano cheese, grated
2 tsp garlic powder
1 tsp onion powder
Salt and black pepper to taste
4 oz ham, sliced
4 oz mozzarella cheese, sliced

Directions

Arrange the chicken slices in a greased baking dish and season with salt and black pepper.

In a bowl, mix mustard, mayonnaise, and erythritol. Spread this mixture over the chicken. Cover the chicken with the Grana-Padano, pork rinds, and seasonings. Place in the oven for about 40 minutes at 350°F until the chicken is cooked completely.

Take out from the oven and top with mozzarella and ham slices. Place back in the oven and cook until golden brown.

Turkey Bacon & Broccoli Pancakes

Total Time: 40 minutes | Serves: 6

Per serving: Calories 454, Fat 32g; Net Carbs 2.4g; Protein 25g

Ingredients

4 eggs
1 head broccoli, cut into florets
1 cup mascarpone, at room temperature
1 tsp xylitol
1½ tbsp almond flour
⅓ cup Parmesan cheese, grated
A pinch of xanthan gum
8 oz mushrooms, sliced
12 turkey bacon slices, cubed
½ cup mozzarella cheese
1 garlic clove, minced
1 onion, chopped
2 tbsp red wine vinegar
2 tbsp olive oil
½ cup heavy cream
¼ cup chicken stock
A pinch of nutmeg
Fresh parsley, chopped
Salt and black pepper, to taste

Directions

Combine 3/4 cup of mascarpone, eggs, xylitol, almond flour, xanthan gum, Parmesan cheese to obtain a crepe batter. Set a pan sprayed with cooking spray over medium heat, pour some of the batter, spread well into the pan, cook for 2 minutes, flip to the other side, and cook for 40 seconds more or until golden. Do the same with the rest of the batter, greasing the pan with cooking spray between each one. Stack all the crepes on a serving plate.

In the same pan, warm the olive oil and stir in the onion and garlic; sauté for 3 minutes, until tender. Stir in the mushrooms and cook for 5 minutes.

Add in the turkey bacon, salt, vinegar, heavy cream, remaining mascarpone, nutmeg, black pepper, broccoli, and stock, and cook for 7 minutes. Fill each crepe with this mixture, roll up each one, and arrange on a baking dish. Scatter over the mozzarella cheese, set under a preheated broiler for 5 minutes. Set the crepes on serving plates; garnish with chopped parsley.

Zucchini Noodles with Turkey & Bolognese Sauce

Total Time: 30 minutes | Serves: 5

Per serving: Calories 273, Fat: 16g; Net Carbs: 3.8g; Protein: 19g

Ingredients

2 cups cremini mushrooms, sliced
1 onion, chopped
2 tsp olive oil
1 pound ground turkey
3 tbsp pesto sauce
1 head broccoli, cut into florets
3 zucchinis, spiralized

Directions

In a skillet over medium heat, warm the olive oil. Add zucchini and cook for 2-3 minutes, stirring continuously; set aside.

To the same oil, add ground turkey and cook until browned, about 7-8 minutes. Transfer to a plate. Add onion and cook until translucent, about 3 minutes. Add broccoli and mushrooms, and cook for 7 more minutes. Return the turkey to the skillet. Stir in the pesto sauce. Cover the pan, lower the heat, and simmer for 15 minutes. Stir in zucchini pasta and serve immediately.

Spanish Chicken with Tomate Sofrito Sauce

Total Time: 40 minutes | Serves: 4

Per serving: Calories 415, Fat 33g; Net Carbs 4g; Protein 25g

Ingredients

½ pound mushrooms, chopped
2 tbsp olive oil
2 red piquillo peppers, seeded, chopped
1 onion, peeled and sliced
2 garlic cloves, minced
14 oz canned tomatoes, chopped
1 pound chicken thighs
Salt and black pepper, to taste
½ cup chicken stock
1 tsp turmeric
2 tsp dried oregano
Fresh parsley, chopped for serving

Directions

Set a pan over medium heat and warm the olive oil, stir in the chicken thighs, and apply pepper and salt for seasoning. Cook each side for 3 minutes and set aside.

In the same pan, add the onion, piquillo peppers, garlic, and mushrooms, and cook for 4 minutes. Pour in the stock, turmeric, salt, tomatoes, pepper, and oregano. Stir in the chicken, place everything to the oven at 400°F, and bake for 30 minutes. Garnish with chopped parsley to serve.

Baby Spinach and Cheese Stuffed Chicken Breasts

Total Time: 50 minutes | Serves: 4

Per serving: Calories 491, Fat: 36g; Net Carbs: 3.5g; Protein: 38g

Ingredients

1 pound chicken breasts, boneless
½ cup ricotta cheese
½ cup mozzarella cheese
⅓ cup Parmesan cheese

Breading:
2 tbsp olive oil
2 eggs
⅓ cup almond flour

2 cups organic baby spinach, chopped
A pinch of nutmeg
1 garlic clove, minced

½ tsp parsley
⅓ cup Parmesan cheese
A pinch of onion powder

Directions

Pound the chicken until it doubles in size. Mix the ricotta cheese, spinach, mozzarella, nutmeg, salt, pepper, and parmesan in a bowl. Divide the mixture between the chicken breasts and spread it out evenly. Wrap the chicken in a plastic wrap. Refrigerate for 15 minutes.

Preheat the oven to 370°F. Beat the eggs and combine all other breading ingredients in a bowl. Heat the oil in a pan. Dip the chicken in egg first, then in the breading mixture. Cook in the pan until browned. Place on a lined baking sheet and bake for 20 minutes.

Four-Cheese Chicken with Pancetta and Zucchini

Total Time: 35 minutes | Serves: 8

Per serving: Calories 565, Fat 37g; Net Carbs 2g; Protein 51g

Ingredients

2 oz fresh mozzarella cheese, cubed
2 oz ricotta cheese, crumbled
4 oz mozzarella cheese, shredded
2 oz provolone cheese, cubed
3 pounds 4 chicken breasts, halved
1 zucchini, shredded
Salt and black pepper, to taste
1 garlic clove, minced
4 oz pancetta, cooked and crumbled

Directions

In a bowl, mix pancetta, zucchini, ricotta, mozzarella cheese, provolone cheese, fresh mozzarella, black pepper, salt, and garlic. Cut slits into chicken breasts, apply pepper and salt, and stuff with cheese mixture. Set on a lined baking sheet, place in the oven at 400°F, and bake for 30 minutes.

Sautééed Pork Lettuce Cup Wraps

Total Time: 20 minutes | Serves: 6

Per serving: Calories 311, Fat 24.3g; Net Carbs 1g; Protein 19g

Ingredients

2 pounds ground pork
2 garlic cloves, minced
Salt and chili pepper to taste
1 tsp olive oil
1 head Iceberg lettuce
1 cucumber, chopped
2 sprigs green onion, chopped
1 bell pepper, seeded and chopped

Directions

Warm olive oil in a saucepan over medium heat and cook the pork with garlic, salt, and chili pepper for 10-15 minutes while breaking any lumps until the pork is no longer pink; turn the heat off.

Pat the lettuce dry with paper towel and in each leaf spoon two to three tablespoons of pork, top with green onions, bell pepper, and cucumber.

Greek-Style Chicken with Olives and Capers

Total Time: 30 minutes | Serves: 4

Per serving: Calories 387, Fat 21g; Net Carbs 2.2g; Protein 25g

Ingredients

3 tbsp olive oil
1 white onion, chopped
1 lb chicken breasts, skinless and boneless
4 garlic cloves, minced
Salt and black pepper, to taste
½ cup kalamata olives, pitted and chopped
1 tbsp capers
4 tomatoes, chopped
½ tsp red chili flakes

Directions

Warm olive oil in a skillet over medium heat and cook the chicken for 2 minutes per side. Sprinkle with black pepper and salt. Set the chicken breasts in the oven at 450°F and bake for 8 minutes. Arrange the chicken on a platter.

In the same pan over medium heat, add the onion, olives, capers, garlic, and chili flakes, and cook for 1 minute. Stir in the tomatoes, pepper, and salt, and cook for 2 minutes. Sprinkle over the chicken breasts and enjoy.

Speedy Tilapia with Tomato Sauce & Olives

Total Time: 16 minutes | Serves: 4

Per serving: Calories 282, Fat: 15g; Net Carbs: 6g; Protein: 23g

Ingredients

1 pound tilapia fillets
2 garlic cloves, minced
14 oz diced tomatoes
1 tbsp olive oil
1 sweet onion, chopped
2 tbsp parsley
12 kalamata olives

Directions

Heat the olive oil in a skillet over medium heat and cook the onion and garlic for about 3 minutes. Stir in tomatoes and bring the mixture to a boil. Reduce the heat and simmer for 5 minutes. Add olives and tilapia. Cook for 8 minutes. Serve the tilapia with tomato sauce.

Minty Pork Balls with Fresh Salad

Total Time: 25 minutes | Serves: 5

Per serving: Calories 408, Fat 22.4g; Net Carbs 8.3g; Protein 27g

Ingredients

2 pounds ground pork
¼ cup almond milk
1 egg, whisked
1 onion, chopped
5 zero carb bread slices, torn
Salt and black pepper, to taste
2 garlic cloves, minced

¼ cup fresh mint, chopped
¼ cup olive oil
1 cup cherry tomatoes, halved
1 cucumber, sliced
16 oz arugula
1½ tbsp lemon juice
1 cup dilled Greek yogurt

Directions

Place the torn bread in a bowl, add in the almond milk, and set aside for 3 minutes. Squeeze the bread, chop, and place into a bowl. Stir in the beef, salt, mint, onion, black pepper, egg, and garlic.

Form balls out of this mixture and place on a working surface. Set a pan over medium heat and warm half of the oil; fry the meatballs for 8 minutes. Flip occasionally, and set aside in a tray.

In a salad plate, combine the arugula with the cherry tomatoes and cucumber. Mix in the remaining oil, lemon juice, black pepper, and salt. Spread dilled yogurt over, and top with meatballs to serve.

Traditional Bolognese Sauce

Total Time: 35 minutes | Serves: 6

Per serving: Calories 318, Fat: 20g; Net Carbs: 5.9g; Protein: 26g

Ingredients

1 onion, chopped
1½ pounds ground beef
2 garlic cloves, minced
1 tsp marjoram

1 tsp rosemary
4 tomatoes, chopped
1 tbsp olive oil

Directions

Heat olive oil in a saucepan over medium heat. Add onion and garlic and cook for 3 minutes. Add beef and cook until browned, about 4-5 minutes. Stir in the herbs and tomatoes. Cook for 15 minutes.

Baked Zucchini Stuffed with Shrimp & Dill

Total Time: 56 minutes | Serves: 4

Per serving: Calories 135, Fat 14.4g; Net Carbs 3.2g; Protein 24.6g

Ingredients

2 tbsp olive oil
20 oz medium zucchinis
1 lb small shrimp, peeled, deveined
½ onion, minced
2 tsp butter
2 tomatoes, chopped
Salt and black pepper to taste
1 cup pork rinds, crushed
1 tbsp fresh dill, chopped

Directions

Trim off the top and bottom ends of the zucchinis. Lay them flat on a chopping board, and cut a ¼-inch off the top to create a boat for the stuffing. Scoop out the seeds with a spoon and set the zucchinis aside.

Melt the butter in a small skillet and sauté the onion and tomato for 6 minutes. Transfer the mixture to a bowl and add the shrimp, half of the pork rinds, fresh dill, salt, and pepper.

Combine the ingredients and stuff the zucchini boats with the mixture. Sprinkle the top of the boats with the remaining pork rinds and drizzle the olive oil over them.

Place on a baking sheet and bake them for 15 to 20 minutes at 350°F. The shrimp should no longer be pink by this time. Remove the zucchinis after and serve with a tomato and mozzarella salad.

Garlic Chicken with Anchovy Paste

Total Time: 30 minutes | Serves: 2

Per serving: Calories 155, Fat 13g; Net Carbs 3g; Protein 25g

Ingredients

½ pound chicken breast, cut into 4 pieces
2 tbsp olive oil
For the paste
1 cup black olives, pitted
4 anchovy fillets, rinsed
1 garlic clove, crushed
Salt and black pepper, to taste

3 garlic cloves, crushed

2 tbsp olive oil
¼ cup fresh basil, chopped
1 tbsp lemon juice

Directions

Using a food processor, combine the olives, salt, olive oil, basil, lemon juice, anchovy fillets, and pepper, blend well. Set a pan over medium heat and warm olive oil, stir-fry in the garlic and chicken and cook for 10 minutes. Remove to a serving plate and top with anchovy paste to serve.

Sardines Skillet with Zucchini Spaghetti

Total Time: 10 minutes | Serves: 2

Per serving: Calories 355, Fat: 31g; Net Carbs: 6g; Protein: 20g

Ingredients

32 oz zucchini spaghetti
2 oz cubed pancetta
4 oz canned sardines, chopped
½ cup canned tomatoes, chopped

4 green olives, pitted and chopped
1 tbsp parsley
1 garlic clove, minced

Directions

Pour some of the sardine oil in a skillet. Add garlic and cook for 1 minute. Add pancetta and cook for 2 minutes. Stir in the tomatoes and let simmer for 5 minutes. Add zucchini spaghetti and sardines and cook for 3 minutes. Remove to a platter and scatter the green olives on top to serve.

Buttered Garlic Shrimp

Total Time: 22 minutes | Serves: 6

Per serving: Calories 258, Fat 22g; Net Carbs 2g; Protein 13g

Ingredients

4 oz butter
2 lb shrimp, peeled and deveined
Sea salt and black pepper to taste
A pinch of red pepper flakes

3 garlic cloves, minced
3 tbsp water
1 lemon, zested and juiced
2 tbsp fresh parsley, chopped

Directions

Warm half of the butter in a large skillet over medium heat, season the shrimp with salt, pepper, pepper flakes, and add to the butter. Stir in the garlic and cook the shrimp for 4 minutes on both sides until pink. Remove to a bowl and set aside.

Put the remaining butter in the skillet; include the lemon zest, juice, and water. Cook until the butter has melted, about 1 minute. Add the shrimp and adjust the taste with salt and black pepper. Cook for 2 minutes on low heat. Serve the shrimp sprinkled with parsley.

Cheesy Salmon with Crème Fraîche Spread

Total Time: 25 minutes | Serves: 4

Per serving: Calories 463, Fat 34.5g; Net Carbs 0g; Protein 33.3g

Ingredients

1 cup crème fraîche
½ tbsp dill, minced
½ lemon, zested and juiced

Sea salt and black pepper to season
1 pound salmon steaks
½ cup Parmesan cheese, grated

Directions

Line a baking sheet with parchment paper; set aside. In a bowl, mix the crème fraîche, dill, lemon zest, juice, salt, and pepper, and set aside. Season the fish with salt and black pepper, drizzle lemon juice on both sides of the fish and arrange them in the baking sheet. Spread the crème fraîche mixture on each fish and sprinkle with Parmesan cheese.

Bake the fish in the oven for 15 minutes at 400°F and after broil the top for 2 minutes with a close watch for a nice a brown color. Plate the fish and serve with buttery green beans.

MEATLESS MEALS

Goat Cheese Frittata with Bell Peppers

Total Time: 17 minutes | Serves: 4

Per serving: Calories 153, Fat 10.3g; Net Carbs 2.3g; Protein 6.4g

Ingredients

4 red chilies, roasted and seeded
2 bell peppers, seeded and chopped
2 tbsp vinegar
8 eggs
4 tbsp olive oil
½ cup Parmesan cheese, grated
¼ cup goat cheese, crumbled
4 cloves garlic, minced
1 head Iceberg lettuce, torn
2 tbsp fresh parsley, chopped

Directions

Cut the chilies into long strips, and pour into a bowl. Mix in the vinegar, half of the parsley, half of the olive oil, and garlic; set aside. In another bowl, whisk the eggs with salt, black pepper, bell peppers, parmesan cheese, and the remaining parsley.

Heat the remaining oil over medium heat and pour the egg mixture along with half of the goat cheese. Cook for 3 minutes and when it is near done, sprinkle the remaining goat cheese on it; transfer the cast iron to the oven. Bake the frittata in the oven for 4 minutes at 400°F, remove and drizzle with the chili oil. Garnish with lettuce salad to serve.

Creamy Vegetable Stew

Total Time: 32 minutes | Serves: 4

Per serving: Calories 310, Fat 26.4g; Net Carbs 6g; Protein 8g

Ingredients

2 tbsp olive oil
1½ cups crème fraîch
1 onion, chopped
1 garlic clove, minced
2 carrots, chopped
1 head cauliflower, cut into florets
2 cups green beans, halved
Salt and black pepper to taste
1 cup water

Directions

Warm olive oil in a saucepan over medium heat and sauté garlic and onion to be fragrant, about 3 minutes.

Stir in carrots, cauliflower, and green beans, salt, and pepper, add the water, stir again, and cook the vegetables on low heat for 25 minutes to soften. Mix in the heavy cream to be incorporated, turn the heat off, and adjust the taste with salt and pepper. Serve the stew with almond flour bread.

Spinach & Feta Lasagna

Total Time: 50 minutes | Serves: 4

Per serving: Calories 390, Fat 39g; Net Carbs 2g; Protein 7g

Ingredients

2 pounds zucchinis, sliced
Salt and black pepper to taste
2 cups feta cheese, crumbled

2 cups mozzarella cheese, shredded
24 oz canned tomato sauce
8 oz baby spinach

Directions

Grease a baking dish with cooking spray. Mix the feta, mozzarella, salt, and pepper to evenly combine and spread ¼ cup of the mixture in the bottom of the baking dish.

Layer ⅓ of the zucchini slices on top spread 1 cup of tomato sauce over, and scatter a ⅓ of the spinach on top. Repeat the layering process two more times to exhaust the ingredients while making sure to layer with the last ¼ cup of cheese mixture finally.

Grease one end of foil with cooking spray and cover the baking dish with the foil. Bake in the oven for 35 minutes at 370°F, remove foil, and bake further for 5 to 10 minutes or until the cheese has a nice golden brown color.

Remove the dish, sit for 5 minutes, make slices of the lasagna, and serve warm.

Eggplant Dipped Roasted Asparagus

Total Time: 35 minutes | Serves: 6

Per serving: Calories 149; Fat: 12.1g; Net Carbs: 9g; Protein: 3.6g

Ingredients

4 tbsp olive oil
1½ pounds asparagus spears, trimmed
For Eggplant Dip
¾ pound eggplants
2 tsp olive oil
½ cup scallions, chopped
2 cloves garlic, minced

Sea salt and black pepper, to taste
½ tsp sweet paprika

1 tbsp lemon juice
½ tsp chili pepper
Salt and black pepper, to taste
Fresh parsley, chopped for garnish

Directions

Line a parchment paper to a baking sheet. Add asparagus spears to the baking sheet. Toss with oil, sweet paprika, black pepper, and salt. Bake in the oven until cooked through for 9 minutes at 390°F.

Add eggplants on a lined cookie sheet. Place under the broiler for about 20 minutes at 425°F; let the eggplants to cool. Peel them and discard the stems. Place a frying pan over medium-high heat and warm olive oil. Add in garlic and onion and sauté until tender.

Using a food processor, pulse together black pepper, roasted eggplants, salt, lemon juice, scallion mixture, and chili pepper to mix evenly. Add parsley for garnishing. Serve alongside roasted asparagus spears.

Steamed Asparagus & Grilled Cauliflower Steaks

Total Time: 20 minutes | Serves: 4

Per serving: Calories 118, Fat 9g; Net Carbs 4g; Protein 2g

Ingredients

4 tbsp olive oil
2 heads cauliflower, sliced into 'steaks'
1 red onion, sliced
¼ cup chili sauce
2 tsp xylitol

Salt and black pepper to taste
1 pound asparagus, trimmed
Juice of 1 lemon
1 cup water
Dried parsley to garnish

Directions

Preheat the grill.

In a bowl, mix the olive oil, chili sauce, and xylitol. Brush the cauliflower with the mixture. Place them on the grill, and cook for 6 minutes. Flip the cauliflower, grill further for 6 minutes.

Bring the water to boil over high heat, place the asparagus in a sieve and set over the steam from the boiling water. Cook for 6 minutes. After, remove to a bowl and toss with lemon juice. Remove the grilled caulis to a plate; sprinkle with salt, black pepper, red onion, and parsley. Serve with the steamed asparagus.

Green Bell Pepper & Mushroom Stew

Total Time: 25 minutes | Serves: 4

Per serving: Calories 114; Fat: 7.3g; Net Carbs: 9.5g; Protein: 2.1g

Ingredients

2 tbsp olive oil
1 onion, chopped
2 garlic cloves, pressed
½ stalk celery, chopped
2 carrots, chopped
8 oz wild mushrooms, sliced
2 tbsp dry white wine
1 thyme sprig, chopped
4 cups vegetable stock
½ tsp chili pepper
1 tsp paprika
2 tomatoes, chopped
1 tbsp flax seed meal

Directions

Warm oil in a stockpot over medium heat. Add in onion and cook until tender.

Place in carrots, celery, and garlic and cook until soft for 4 more minutes. Add in mushrooms; cook the mixture the liquid is lost; set the vegetables aside. Stir in wine to deglaze the stockpot's bottom. Place in thyme.

Pour in tomatoes, vegetable stock, paprika, and chili pepper; add in reserved vegetables and allow to boil.

On low heat, allow the mixture to simmer for 15 minutes while covered. Stir in the flax seed meal to thicken the stew. Plate into individual bowls and serve.

Mushroom Cheeseburgers

Total Time: 15 minutes | Serves: 4

Per serving: Calories 190, Fat 8g; Net Carbs 3g; Protein 16g

Ingredients

8 portobello mushroom caps
1 clove garlic
Salt to taste
2 tbsp olive oil
½ cup roasted red peppers, sliced
14 oz canned tomatoes, chopped
¼ cup feta cheese, crumbled
1 tbsp red wine vinegar
2 tbsp kalamata olives, pitted and chopped
½ tsp dried oregano
2 cups baby salad greens

Directions

Crush the garlic with salt in a bowl using the back of a spoon. Stir in 1 tbsp of oil and brush the mushrooms with the mixture. Heat the grill pan over medium heat and place in the mushrooms; grill them on both sides for 8 minutes until tender.

In a bowl, mix the red peppers, tomatoes, olives, feta cheese, vinegar, oregano, baby salad greens, and remaining oil; toss them. Assemble the burger: scoop the cheese mixture into 4 mushroom caps and top with the remaining caps.

Traditional Spanish Pisto

Total Time: 47 minutes | Serves: 6

Per serving: Calories 154, Fat 12.1g; Net Carbs 5.6g; Protein 1.7g

Ingredients

6 eggs
3 zucchinis, chopped
2 eggplants, chopped
2 onions, diced
Zest of ½ lemon
28 oz canned tomatoes
2 red bell peppers, cut in chunks
1 yellow bell pepper, cut in chunks
3 cloves garlic, sliced
4 sprigs thyme
1 tbsp balsamic vinegar
3 tbsp olive oil

Directions

Warm 1 tbsp of olive oil and fry the eggs; remove to a platter, cover with aluminium foil to keep warm and set aside.

In a casserole pot, heat the remaining olive oil and sauté the eggplants, zucchinis, and bell peppers over medium heat for 5 minutes. Spoon the veggies into a large bowl.

In the same pan, sauté garlic, onions, and thyme leaves for 5 minutes and return the cooked veggies to the pan along with the canned tomatoes, balsamic vinegar, chopped basil, salt, and pepper to taste. Stir and cover the pot, cook the ingredients on low heat for 30 minutes.

Open the lid and stir in the remaining basil leaves, lemon zest, and adjust the seasoning. Turn the heat off. Plate the ratatouille and serve with fried eggs.

Green Beans & Sage Flan

Total Time: 65 minutes | Serves: 4

Per serving: Calories 264, Fat 11.6g; Net Carbs 2.5g; Protein 12.5g

Ingredients

1 cup green beans, ends removed
½ cup whipping cream
1 cup almond milk
2 eggs + 2 egg yolks, beaten in a bowl
2 tbsp fresh sage, chopped
Salt and black pepper to taste

A small pinch of nutmeg
2 tbsp Parmesan cheese, grated
4 cups water
2 tbsp butter, melted
1 tbsp butter, softened

Directions

Pour 1 cup of the water and some salt in a pot, add the green beans, and bring to boil over medium heat for 6 minutes. Drain the green beans, and chop into small pieces.

In a blender, add the chopped green beans, whipping cream, almond milk, sage, salt, nutmeg, black pepper, and Parmesan cheese. Process the ingredients on high speed until smooth. Pour the mixture through a sieve into a bowl and whisk the eggs into it.

Preheat the oven to 350°F. Grease the ramekins with softened butter and share the green bean mixture among the ramekins. Pour the melted butter over each mixture. Pour the remaining water into a baking dish, place in the ramekins, and insert in the oven.

Bake for 45 minutes until their middle parts are no longer watery. Remove the ramekins and let cool.

Classic Greek Salad with Dill Dressing

Total Time: 3 hrs 15 minutes | Serves: 4

Per serving: Calories 208; Fat: 15.6g; Net Carbs: 6.7g; Protein: 7.6g

Ingredients

For the Dressing

2 tbsp green onions, chopped
2 cups water
1 garlic clove, minced
½ lemon, freshly squeezed

Salt and black pepper, to taste
¼ tsp dill, minced
2 tbsp almond milk

For the salad

1 head lettuce, torn
3 tomatoes, diced
3 cucumbers, sliced

2 tbsp kalamata olives, pitted
4 oz feta cheese, crumbled

Directions

In a large bowl, mix the lettuce, olives, red onion, tomato, cucumber, and feta. Put all dressing ingredients in a food processor and pulse until well incorporated. Add the dressing to the salad and shake.

Zucchini Spaghetti with Avocado & Capers

Total Time: 15 minutes | Serves: 4

Per serving: Calories 449, Fat: 42g; Net Carbs: 8.4g; Protein: 6.3g

Ingredients

2 tbsp olive oil
1 pound zucchinis, julienned
½ cup pesto

2 avocados, sliced
½ cup capers
¼ cup sun-dried tomatoes, chopped

Directions

Heat half of the olive oil in a pan over medium heat. Add zucchinis and cook for 4 minutes. Transfer to a plate. Stir in pesto, salt, tomatoes, and capers. Top with avocado slices.

Vegan Minestrone

Total Time: 25 minutes | Serves: 5

Per serving: Calories 227, Fat 20.3g; Net Carbs 2g; Protein 8g

Ingredients

2 tbsp olive oil
1 small onion, chopped
1 garlic clove, minced
2 heads broccoli, cut in florets
2 stalks celery, chopped
5 cups vegetable broth
1 cup baby spinach
Salt and black pepper to taste

Directions

Sauté the onion and garlic in a saucepan over medium heat for 3 minutes until softened. Mix in broccoli and celery, and cook for 4 minutes until slightly tender. Pour in broth, bring to a boil, then reduce the heat to medium-low and simmer covered for about 5 minutes.

Drop in the spinach to wilt, adjust the seasonings, and cook for 4 minutes. Ladle soup into bowls and serve.

Cauliflower & Kale Cheese Waffles

Total Time: 45 minutes | Serves: 3

Per serving: Calories 283, Fat: 20.2g; Net Carbs: 3.6g; Protein: 16g

Ingredients

2 spring onions, chopped
1 tbsp olive oil
2 eggs
⅓ cup Parmesan cheese
8 oz kale, chopped
1 cup mozzarella cheese, shredded
½ cauliflower head
1 tsp garlic powder
1 tbsp sesame seeds
2 tsp rosemary, chopped

Directions

Place the chopped cauliflower in the food processor and process until rice is formed. Add kale, spring onions, and rosemary to the food processor. Pulse until smooth. Transfer to a bowl. Stir in the rest of the ingredients and mix to combine.

Heat waffle iron and spread in ¼ of the mixture, evenly. Cook until golden, about 3 minutes. Repeat with the remaining batter.

Classic Pizza Margherita the Keto Way

Total Time: 40 minutes | Serves: 2

Per serving: Calories 510, Fat: 39g; Net Carbs: 3.7g; Protein: 31g

Ingredients

1 cup mozzarella cheese, shredded
2 tbsp mascarpone, at room temperature
2 tbsp Parmesan cheese, grated

1 tsp oregano
½ cup almond flour
2 tbsp psyllium husk

Topping

4 ounces mozzarella cheese, grated
¼ cup Marinara sauce
1 bell pepper, sliced

1 tomato, sliced
2 tbsp basil, chopped

Directions

Combine mascarpone, parmesan cheese, oregano, almond flour, and psyllium husk in a large bowl.

Melt the mozzarella in a microwave. Stir it into the bowl. Mix with your hands to combine. Divide the dough in two. Roll out the two crusts in circles and place on a lined baking sheet. Bake in the oven for about 10 minutes at 400°F. Top with the topping. Return to the oven and bake for another 10 minutes.

Charred Asparagus with Creamy Sauce

Total Time: 11 minutes | Serves: 4

Per serving: Calories: 520g; Fat: 53g; Net Carbs: 6g; Protein: 6.3g

Ingredients

Flax Egg

4 tbsp flax seed powder + ½ cup water
4 tbsp olive oil
1 cup mozzarella cheese, grated

½ cup heavy cream
Salt and powdered chili pepper to taste

Asparagus

1 tbsp olive oil
½ lb asparagus, hard stalks removed
Salt and black pepper to taste

⅓ cup butter
Juice of ½ lemon

Directions

To make the flax egg: in a safe microwave bowl, mix the flax seed powder with water and set aside to thicken for 5 minutes.

Warm the flax egg in the microwave for 1 minute, then, pour into a blender. Add the olive oil, mozzarella cheese, heavy cream, salt, and chili pepper. Puree the ingredients until well combined and smooth.

Heat 1 tbsp of the olive oil in a saucepan and roast the asparagus until lightly charred. Season with salt and black pepper, set aside.

Melt the butter in a frying pan until nutty and golden brown. Stir in the lemon juice and pour the mixture into a sauce cup. Spoon the creamy blend into the center of four serving plates and use the back of the spoon to spread out lightly. Top with the asparagus and drizzle the lemon butter on top.

White Cabbage with Parmesan

Total Time: 25 minutes | Serves: 4

Per serving: Calories 268, Fat 19.3g; Net Carbs 4g; Protein 17.5g

Ingredients

4 tbsp olive oil
1 large head white cabbage, cut into wedges
1 garlic clove, minced
Salt and black pepper to taste
1 cup Parmesan cheese, grated
Parmesan cheese, grated for topping
1 tbsp parsley, chopped to garnish

Directions

Line a baking sheet with foil, and grease with cooking spray. Mix the olive oil, garlic, salt, and black pepper until evenly combined. Brush the mixture on all sides of the cabbage wedges and sprinkle with parmesan cheese.

Place on the baking sheet, and bake in the oven for 20 minutes at 400°F to soften the cabbage and melt the cheese.

Remove the cabbages when golden brown, sprinkle with extra cheese and parsley.

Cauliflower Patties

Total Time: 15 minutes | Serves: 4

Per serving: Calories 315, Fat 26g; Net Carbs 2g; Protein 8g

Ingredients

4 tbsp olive oil
1 head cauliflower, cut into florets
⅓ cup silvered ground almonds
½ tsp Italian seasoning

Salt and chili pepper to taste
3 tbsp almond flour
3 eggs

Directions

Puree the cauli florets in a food processor until a grain meal consistency is formed. Pour the puree in a bowl, add the ground almonds, Italian seasoning, salt, chili pepper, and almond flour, and mix until combined.

Beat the eggs in a bowl until creamy in color and mix with the cauli mixture. Shape ¼ cup each into patties.

Warm olive oil in a frying pan over medium heat and fry the patties for 5 minutes on each side to be firm and browned. Remove onto a wire rack to cool, share into serving plates, and serve.

Tumeric Baked Vegetables

Total Time: 40 minutes | Serves: 4

Per serving: Calories 390; Fat: 23.1g; Net Carbs: 8.6g; Protein: 24.4g

Ingredients

½ pound parsnip, sliced
2 bell peppers, sliced
2 tbsp olive oil
1 onion, chopped
½ stick celery, chopped
2 carrots, grated

1 cup vegetable broth
1 tsp turmeric
Sea salt and black pepper, to taste
½ tsp liquid smoke
1 cup Parmesan cheese, shredded
2 tbsp fresh chives, chopped

Directions

Grease a baking dish with olive oil. Set a skillet over medium heat and warm olive oil. Sweat the onion until soft. Place in the parsnip slices, carrots, bell peppers, and celery. Cook for 4 minutes.

Remove the vegetable mixture to the baking dish. Combine vegetable broth with turmeric, black pepper, liquid smoke, and salt. Spread this mixture over the vegetables. Scatter parmesan cheese over the top and bake in the oven for about 30 minutes at 360°F. Decorate with fresh chives and serve.

Cheesy Spaghetti Squash

Total Time: 40 minutes | Serves: 4

Per serving: Calories: 515; Fat: 45g; Net Carbs: 7g; Protein: 18g

Ingredients

2 lb spaghetti squash, halved and seeded
3 tbsp olive oil
Salt and black pepper to taste
½ tbsp garlic powder
1/5 tsp chili powder
1 cup heavy cream
4 tbsp mascarpone
1 cup mozzarella cheese, shredded
4 tbsp parmesan cheese, shredded
2 tbsp fresh parsley, chopped

Directions

Place the halves, cut-side down, on a baking dish, brush each with 1 tbsp of the olive oil, and season with salt and black pepper. Bake in the oven for 40 minutes at 350°F or until the pulp has softened.

Remove the squash and leave to cool slightly. Use 2 forks to shred the flesh into strands. Empty the spaghetti strands into a bowl and mix with the remaining olive oil, garlic powder, chili powder, heavy cream, mascarpone, half of the mozzarella cheese, and the parmesan cheese.

Spoon the mixture into the squash cups and sprinkle with the remaining mozzarella cheese. Bake for 5 minutes or until the cheese is golden brown. Season with pepper, parsley, and drizzle with some olive oil.

Vegan Cheese Stuffed Zucchini

Total Time: 38 minutes | Serves: 2

Per serving: Calories: 620; Fat: 57g; Net Carbs: 4g; Protein: 20g

Ingredients

2 zucchinis, halved
4 tbsp olive oil
2 garlic cloves, minced
1½ oz baby arugula

Salt and black pepper to taste
2 tbsp tomato sauce, sugar-free
1 cup vegan Parmesan cheese, shredded

Directions

Scoop out the pulp of the zucchinis into a plate. Keep the flesh. Grease a baking sheet with cooking spray and place in the zucchini halves.

Warm the olive oil in a skillet over medium heat. Add and sauté the garlic until fragrant, about 1 minute. Add the arugula and zucchini pulp. Cook until the arugula wilts; season with salt and pepper. Spoon the tomato sauce into the boats and spread to coat the bottom.

Then, spoon the arugula mixture into the zucchinis and sprinkle with the vegan parmesan cheese. Bake in the oven for 20 to 25 minutes at 370°F or until the cheese has a beautiful golden color. Plate the zucchinis when ready, season with salt and black pepper. .

Kale & Cauliflower Soup

Total Time: 15 minutes | Serves: 4

Per serving: Calories 172; Fat: 10.3g; Net Carbs: 11.8g; Protein: 8.1g

Ingredients

2 tbsp olive oil
1 onion, chopped
1 garlic clove, minced
1 head cauliflower, cut into florets
8 oz kale, chopped

4 cups vegetable broth
½ cup almond milk
Salt to taste
½ tsp red pepper flakes
1 tbsp fresh parsley, chopped

Directions

Warm the olive oil in a pot over medium-high heat. Add garlic and onion and sauté until browned and softened, about 3 minutes.

Place in vegetable broth, kale, and cauliflower; cook for 10 minutes until the mixture boils. Stir in the pepper, salt, and almond milk; simmer the soup while covered for 5 minutes.

Transfer the soup to an immersion blender and blend to achieve the required consistency; top with parsley and serve.

Creamy Avocado Carbonara

Total Time: 30 minutes | Serves: 4

Per serving: Calories: 870; Fat: 69g; Net Carbs: 8g; Protein: 35g

Ingredients

8 tbsp flax seed powder + 1½ cups water
1½ cups cream cheese
1 tsp salt
5 ½ tbsp psyllium husk powder
1 avocado, peeled and pitted
1¾ cups heavy cream

½ lemon, juiced
1 tsp onion powder
½ tsp garlic powder
4 tbsp olive oil
Sea salt and black pepper, to taste

For serving

4 tbsp toasted pecans

½ cup Parmesan cheese, grated

Directions

Line a baking sheet with parchment paper

In a medium bowl, mix the flax seed powder with water and allow sitting to thicken for 5 minutes. Add cream cheese, salt, and psyllium husk powder. Whisk until smooth batter forms.

Pour the batter into the prepared baking sheet and cover with another parchment paper. Use a rolling pin to flatten the dough into the sheet. Bake in the oven for 10 to 12 minutes at 300°F.

When ready, slice the pasta into thin strips lengthwise. Cut each piece into halves, pour into a bowl; set aside.

In a blender, combine the avocado, heavy cream, lemon juice, onion powder, and garlic powder. Puree the ingredients until smooth. Pour the olive oil over the pasta and stir to coat properly. Pour the avocado sauce on top and mix. Season with salt, black pepper, and the parmesan cheese. Combine again. Divide the pasta into serving plates, garnish with extra parmesan and pecans to serve.

DESSERTS

Macadamia Ice Cream

Total Time: 3 hours 40 minutes | Serves: 4

Per serving: Calories 302, Fat 32g; Net Carbs 2g; Protein 5g

Ingredients

- 2 cups heavy cream
- 1 tbsp xylitol
- ½ cup macadamia butter, softened
- 1 tbsp olive oil
- ½ tsp salt
- 2 eggs yolks
- ½ cup swerve sweetener confectioners
- ½ cup chopped macadamia nuts

Directions

Melt the heavy cream with macadamia butter, olive oil, xylitol, and salt in a small pan over low heat without boiling about 3 minutes. Remove from the heat.

In a bowl, beat the egg yolks until creamy in color. Stir the eggs into the cream mixture.

Continue stirring until a thick batter has formed; about 3 minutes. Pour the cream mixture into a bowl. Refrigerate for 30 minutes, and stir in swerve sweetener confectioners.

Pour the mixture into ice cream machine and churn it according to the manufacturer's instructions. Stir in the pecans after and spoon the mixture into loaf pan. Freeze for 2 hours before serving.

Cardamom Cookies

Total Time: 25 minutes | Serves: 4

Per serving: Calories 131, Fat: 13g; Net Carbs: 1.5g; Protein: 3g

Ingredients

- 2 cups almond flour
- ½ cup butter, softened
- ½ tsp baking soda
- ¾ cup xylitol
- ½ tsp salt

Coating:

- 2 tbsp xylitol
- 1 tsp cardamom

Directions

Combine almond flour, butter, baking soda, xylitol. and salt in a bowl. Make balls out of the mixture and flatten them with hands. Combine the cardamom and remaining xylitol. Dip the cookies in the cardamom mixture and arrange them on a lined cookie sheet. Cook in the oven for 15 minutes at 350°F, until crispy.

Keto Creme Caramel

Total Time: 10 minutes | Serves: 5

Per serving: Calories 468, Fat: 45.9g; Net Carbs: 4g; Protein: 9.3g

Ingredients

1 egg yolk
5 eggs
2 cups almond milk
⅓ cup erythritol, for caramel

1 tbsp vanilla extract
½ cup erythritol, for custard
2 cup heavy whipping cream

Directions

Start with the caramel: heat the erythritol for the caramel in a deep pan. Add 2-3 tablespoons of water, and bring to a boil. Reduce the heat and cook until the caramel turns golden brown. Divide between 5 metal tins. Let cool.

Preheat the oven to 345°F. In a bowl, mix the eggs, egg yolk, remaining erythritol, lemon zest, and vanilla extract. Add the almond milk and beat again until well combined.

Pour the mixture into each caramel-lined ramekin and place them into a deep baking tin. Fill over the way with the remaining hot water.

Bake for 45-50 minutes. Using tongs, take out the ramekins and let them cool for at least 4 hours in the fridge. Invert onto a dish. Serve with dollops of whipped cream.

Dark Chocolate Hazelnut Chocolate Bark

Total Time: 1 hr 15 minutes | Serves: 12

Per serving: Calories 161, Fat: 15.3g; Net Carbs: 1.9g; Protein: 1.9g

Ingredients

½ cup hazelnut butter
½ cup toasted hazelnuts, chopped
10 drops stevia
¼ tsp salt
4 ounces dark chocolate

Directions

Melt the hazelnut butter and chocolate, in the microwave, for 90 seconds. Remove and stir in stevia.

Line a cookie sheet with waxed paper and spread the chocolate evenly. Scatter the hazelnuts on top and sprinkle with salt. Refrigerate for one hour.

Hazelnut Truffles with Berry

Total Time: 6 min + cooling time | Serves: 8

Per serving: Calories 251, Fat 18.3g; Net Carbs 3.5g; Protein 12g

Ingredients

5 oz unsweetened chocolate chips
1 cup raw hazelnuts
1 tbsp flax seed
¾ cup sugar-free berry preserves
1½ tbsp erythritol
1½ tbsp olive oil

Directions

Grind the hazelnuts and flax seeds in a blender for 45 seconds until smoothly crushed; add the berry and 2 tbsp of erythritol.

Process further for 1 minute until well combined. Form 1-inch balls of the mixture, place on a parchment paper–lined baking sheet, and freeze for 1 hour or until firmed up.

Melt the chocolate chips, oil, and 1tbsp of erythritol in a microwave for 90 seconds. Toss the truffles to coat in the chocolate mixture, put on the baking sheet, and freeze further for at least 2 hours.

Mini Chocolate Cheesecakes

Total Time: 4 min + cooling time | Serves: 6

Per serving: Calories 322, Fat 22g; Net Carbs 13.1g; Protein 13g

Ingredients

½ cup sour cream
1¼ cups mini dark chocolate chips
20 oz mascarpone, at time temperature
½ cup granulated erythritol
1 tsp vanilla extract

Directions

In the microwave, melt the chocolate with sour cream for 1 minute.

In a bowl, whisk the mascarpone, erythritol, and vanilla extract with a hand mixer until smooth. Stir into the chocolate mixture. Spoon into silicone muffin tins and freeze for 4 hours until firm.

Chocolate Pudding in a Mug

Total Time: 10 minutes | Serves: 2

Per serving: Calories 375, Fat 38g; Net Carbs 2.7g; Protein 12g

Ingredients

2 eggs
3 oz almond flour
8 tbsp xylitol
8 tbsp unsweetened cocoa powder
3 oz almond milk
4 tbsp olive oil
½ tsp baking powder
Whipped cream for topping

Directions

Mix almond flour, xylitol, cocoa powder, espresso powder, eggs, coconut milk, olive oil, and baking powder in a bowl. Pour the mix into mugs ¾ way up and cook in a microwave for 70 seconds.

Remove and swirl a generous amount of whipping cream on the cakes and serve.

Fluffy Chocolate Mousse with Strawberries

Total Time: 30 minutes | Serves: 4

Per serving: Calories 192, Fat: 16.4g; Net Carbs: 4.3g; Protein: 5.5g

Ingredients

3 eggs
¼ tsp salt
8 oz dark chocolate, melted
1 cup heavy cream

1 cup fresh strawberries, sliced
1 vanilla extract
1 tbsp xylitol

Directions

In a medium mixing bowl, whip the cream until very soft. Add the eggs, vanilla extract, and xylitol; whisk to combine. Fold int the chocolate.

Divide the mousse between glasses, top with the strawberry slices and chill in the fridge for at least 30 minutes before serving.

Cashew Cakes

Total Time: 25 minutes | Serves: 6

Per serving: Calories 284, Fat: 22.5g; Net Carbs: 2.8g; Protein: 9.9g

Ingredients

1 egg
2 cups ground cashew
¼ cup xylitol

½ tsp baking soda
1 tbsp olive oil
20 walnuts halves

Directions

In a bowl, combine egg, ground cashew, baking soda, and olive oil, and mix well. Make 20 balls out of the mixture and press them with your thumb onto a lined cookie sheet. Top each cookie with a walnut half. Bake for about 12 minutes at 350°F.

Speedy Fat Bombs

Total Time: 3 min + cooling time | Serves: 4

Per serving: Calories 241, Fat 27.1g; Net Carbs 0.2g; Protein J1.5

Ingredients

½ cup almond butter
½ cup olive oil

4 tbsp unsweetened cocoa powder
½ cup xylitol

Directions

Warm butter and olive oil in the microwave for 45 seconds, stirring twice until properly melted and mixed. Mix in cocoa powder and xylitol until completely combined. Pour into muffin molds and refrigerate for 3 hours to harden.

14-DAY MEAL PLAN TO LOSE UP TO 20 POUNDS

Drink 7 to 9 glasses of water daily

Day	Breakfast	Lunch	Dinner	Dessert/Snacks	Kkal
1	Almond Flour Crepes with Rasberry Sauce	Homemade Rolled Porchetta Roast with Pine Nuts	Stuffed Chicken Breasts with Basil Tomato Sauce	Mozzarella Biscuits	1,724
2	Pistachio & Mascarpone pots	Summer Spanish Gazpacho with Ricotta Cheese	French Chicken Packets	Speedy Fat Bombs (x2)	1,722
3	Mozzarella & Chistorra Spanish Chorizo Omelet	Greek Moussaka	Turkey Meatballs with Squash Pasta	Green Bean Crisps	1,843
4	Nut Granola with Yogurt Smoothie	Baked Italian Sausage with Cheese Topping	Greek-Style Chicken with Olives and Capers	Herby Stuffed Eggs	1,842
5	Cheese & Prosciutto Frittata	Parsley Beef Meatballs with Marinara Sauce	Tumeric Baked Vegetables	Keto Creme Caramel	1,980
6	Morning Buttered Eggs	Cauliflower Cream Soup with Pancetta & Chives	Delicious Chicken Goujons	Fluffy Chocolate Mousse with Strawberries	1,971
7	Power Avocado-Berry Smoothie	Juicy Pork Chops with Olives	Chicken Breasts Stuffed with Parma Ham	Macadamia Ice Cream	1,932
8	Cinnamon Waffles with Cheesy Spread	Broccoli Cheese Soup	Mediterranean Chicken Breasts	Hazelnut Truffles with Berry	1,689

9	Egg & Aioli Salad	Spanish Chorizo Chicken Paella	Cheesy Salmon with Crème Fraîche Spread	Cardamom Cookies	1,772
10	Breakfast Almond Milk Shake	Turkey Pizza with Pesto Topping	Grilled Asparagus with Pancetta Wrapped Chicken	Mascarpone & Carrot Mousse	1,948
11	Mozzarella & Broccoli Scramble	Veggie and Pork Osso Bucco	Minty Pork Balls with Fresh Salad	Mini Chocolate Cheesecakes (x2)	1,916
12	Zucchini Patties with Pancetta	Baked Pork Sausages	Omelet Flambé	Mushroom Cheesy Balls	1,735
13	Smoked Salmon & Mascarpone Omelet Roll	Almond-Crusted Salmon	Classic Pizza Margherita the Keto Way	Greek Zucchini Chips	1,709
14	Carrot Zucchini Bread	Minty Pesto Rubbed Pork Chops	Turkey Bacon & Broccoli Pancakes	Cashew Cakes	1,720

Made in the USA
Lexington, KY
23 August 2019